THE MODERN GERMAN NOVEL

UNIVERSITY OF HULL PUBLICATIONS

THE
MODERN GERMAN NOVEL

A MID-TWENTIETH CENTURY SURVEY

BY

H. M. WAIDSON

Published for the UNIVERSITY OF HULL *by the*
OXFORD UNIVERSITY PRESS
LONDON   NEW YORK   TORONTO
1959

Oxford University Press, Amen House, London E.C.4
GLASGOW NEW YORK TORONTO MELBOURNE WELLINGTON
BOMBAY CALCUTTA MADRAS KARACHI KUALA LUMPUR
CAPE TOWN IBADAN NAIROBI ACCRA

Printed in Great Britain

CONTENTS

FOREWORD

MANY friends and colleagues, both in this country and abroad, have helped me with suggestions, references and the loan of books; I should like first of all to express my gratitude to them. Special thanks are due to the staff of the Library of the University of Hull who have borrowed books for me through the National Central Library. The Library of the German Language, London, has also been very helpful. Many of the volumes discussed in the pages that follow are now available in the various university libraries of this country; a number of others have been obtained from libraries in Austria, Germany and Switzerland. Much of the material, of course, is in print at the time of going to press, and obtainable through the usual trade channels.

A certain amount of the text appeared previously in the form of essays and reviews in various journals, for the most part in *German Life and Letters*. The more substantial of these essays are listed in the 'Select Bibliography'.

I am grateful to the Publications Committee of the University of Hull for including this study in its series.

Hull   H. M. WAIDSON
September 1958

I

THE BLURRED EDGES OF REALISM

THE principal aim of the pages that follow is to give an account of prose fiction written in German between 1945 and 1957. The decade which has just passed has been a lively period in the production of novels and shorter stories in Central Europe; moreover, it draws together various phases of the German novel from earlier periods and allows us to examine works which, while being freely open to external influences, whether from England, America, Russia, France, or elsewhere, at the same time have their own peculiar stamp. From this contemporary writing we may legitimately deduce the existence of features which are peculiar to German fiction, and ask where the special contribution of German novelists lies, and what their particular problems are. Before reviewing books that have been written since 1945 it may be apposite to recall tendencies in German imaginative prose writing at earlier periods and their relevance in more recent times.

Much contemporary German writing is concerned with topical issues. Young writers take as their starting-point milieux and situations that have been immediately experienced, while older authors who once kept contemporary references out of their work have shared in the general demand for writing about the present and the immediate past. There is much and obvious commitment to political or religious or philosophical attitudes in contemporary German literature. That this is so will occasion no surprise now, for it may be seen as a reaction against the regimentation of thought that took place during the twelve years of National Socialism. The sheer geography and history of Germany and Austria in the last twenty-five years might indeed justify a classification of writing in German from an ideological point of view. The literature of German-speaking Switzerland in its turn stems from a basis of tradition and relationship to contemporary events which, though different from the outlook of Germany and Austria, nevertheless has much in common with it. In Germany cleavages of opinion have been sharp enough, apart from the shocks and reversals attending ordinary day-to-day life. The war, the collapse of the Nazi régime, the immediate aftermath of war with its conditions of economic chaos, the subsequent regaining of stability and material prosperity, the persisting tension between Russia and the West, the allurements of cellophane, high gloss and concrete, and the threats of total annihilation and the return of chaos at any moment of the day or night—these factors are sufficient cause to accentuate bewilderment and confusion, as also to furnish unprecedented raw material to the novelist.

The extent to which novelists within Germany during the war years were allowed freedom to express themselves has been discussed by H. Boeschenstein in his valuable book *The German Novel 1939-1944* (1949). There was a continued output of competent and, for the most part, though not entirely, undistinguished fiction which carefully avoided discussion of political and topical themes. The occasional references to political tyranny had to be veiled and made less sharp than in the case of Ernst Jünger's *Auf den Marmorklippen* ('On the Marble Cliffs', 1939). Unless one was prepared to write on behalf of the régime, it was safer to avoid all references to the contemporary social scene and to withdraw into non-committal themes. Experimentation with language and narrative techniques was forbidden as a manifestation of 'decadent art'. Apart from the writers who had left Germany as refugees, numerous others were forbidden to publish or else themselves chose not to publish during the twelve years of Hitler's dictatorship. Referring to the novels of the war period, Boeschenstein writes:

In contrast with the style of American fiction, German diction, too often a fabric of clichés, looks faded, washed out. This condition of tepid listlessness cannot possibly be attributed to accident . . . It is not the absence of personal linguistic virtuosity which is to be deplored, but the lack of contact with lively language. Such language is never the creation of one man only, or of a few men; it develops from a healthy emotional, intellectual or occupational group life, from a richly integrated society that is free to air all its concerns frankly.

Although there is a considerable amount of reference to political themes in the German novel since 1945, this is by no means its main concern and problem. Topical events will give an external setting to many present-day German novels, but they cannot determine their ultimate worthwhileness as literature. Since 1945 German writers in the West and Austrian authors have not been faced as previously by totalitarian restrictions on thought and self-expression. But this fact, important perhaps as a prerequisite for the novelist's task of giving a picture of a living world, remains only a prerequisite for the imaginative writer. He must have pen and paper and the indefinable urge to express something with them; he must have the opportunity to say what he has to say to other people. But the existence of a relatively free society is not in itself a guarantee that what he writes will be worthwhile from a literary point of view. This is no doubt obvious, but is stated here in order to make clear that social and political factors are not regarded here as ultimately determining of literary quality, and that even if a number of the books to be mentioned in the following pages may transpire to have primarily a documentary value, it is recognized that the problem of the modern German novel is not a political one in the narrow sense of the word. Once a non-conformity of aesthetic style as well as of personal opinion is granted to the novelist there is a greater possibility of worthwhile literature being produced; but it is no guarantee that this will automatically follow. The ballast of ideas and intellectual discussion in the German novel has traditionally been much greater than in the English or French novel, and this has resulted frequently in a formal discursiveness that is tiresome; it is, however, a factor which is not of final relevance.

One criterion which has frequently and with justification been applied to determine the quality of a novel is the faithfulness of its portrayal of contemporary society. The majority of the great nineteenth-century novels have been realistic; they depict people, places and situations which the reader can readily believe to have been a plausible reconstruction of something that not only the author could see, but that any other percipient person could have witnessed if he had been in comparable circumstances. The imaginative world of Jane Austen is perhaps most completely credible in this sense; sober, dispassionate, sharply observed and cleanly caught, a small social group is mirrored with what convinces us as accuracy. The larger worlds of Dickens, Thackeray and Henry James may be less precisely rendered, but they are pictures of existing societies; there are edges, in Dickens particularly, which blur off into fantasy, but in the main the portrayals are convincing as imitations of things and behaviour which are outside the story-teller. This is true too of Conrad and Bennett, and still true in part of D. H. Lawrence. The nineteenth-century novel in France is distinguished by a similar quality; Balzac, Stendhal and Zola are names which spring to mind in the context of realism, and to these should be added Flaubert, even if there is something more problematic about his relationship to things seen. In Russia there are Turgenev and Tolstoy. The important mid-nineteenth-century German novelists are similarly by and large realists, though of a regional, largely non-urban setting. Gotthelf's work depicts farming communities in Canton Berne, while Keller takes middle-class or lower middle-class Zürich. Similarly Stifter, Storm and Raabe confine themselves to small-scale settings, while Fontane's portrait of Prussian society comes nearer to the wider vistas of the French novel.

German fiction is, however, less firmly rooted in the traditions of realism than is the case with French or English literature. Already the seventeenth-century novel of Grimmelshausen, *Der abenteuerliche Simplicissimus* ('The Adventurous Simplicissimus'), contains many fantastic episodes, while the first important eighteenth-century novel, Wieland's *Agathon*, is set in a tenuously outlined ancient Greek background. Goethe's *Wilhelm Meister* is on the whole a realistic novel, though an unmistakable aura of the daemonic surrounds characters such as Mignon, the Harpist and Makarie; *Die Wahlverwandtschaften* ('Kindred by Choice'), that important novel of married life at the beginning of the nineteenth century, is in the main a psychological study of great penetration, but the analysis is supported by numerous devices of a non-rational character—omens, forebodings, apparent miracles. German Romanticism may have failed in its attempt to make of the novel form a genre which should embrace all aspects of experience, 'Universalpoesie'; the lack of coherence and common-sense plausibility that emerges in the more ambitious narrative prose of Novalis, Brentano, Arnim and others makes one sigh that such good poetry and insight should have been as good as lost to the general reader by the Romantics' reluctance to make artistic use of the world that they were experiencing directly around them. It may willingly be admitted that the novelist who abandons firm hold of the reality around him for the sake of the subjective fantasies of his own mind is running a graver risk of complete artistic failure than the writer who draws mostly upon people and phenomena outside himself. If E. T. A. Hoffmann remains the most readable of the German Romantic writers of fiction, it is because he was able to retain contact with everyday life while letting his narrative leap into situations of wild fantasy. Such a breaking-down of the empirical world is rarer in the French and English novel than in the German, and unusual too in German writing of the mid-nineteenth century. It happens with terrifying impact in Gotthelf's *Die schwarze Spinne* ('The Black Spider'), a masterpiece as exceptional as Emily Brontë's *Wuthering Heights*, and it occurs infrequently and peripherally in some of the writing of Mörike, Stifter and Keller.

At the close of the nineteenth century realism again ceased to be the overwhelmingly dominant form of expression in German fiction. Naturalism in its doctrinaire form was relatively short-lived in Germany, and this movement has left little prose that is outstanding in quality. It was Nietzsche, supported by the example of Schopenhauer and Wagner, who threw the assumptions of the nineteenth-century realists into some confusion and who, no doubt indirectly more often than directly, was responsible for the fragmentation of the novelist's world which has occurred in much of the writing of this century. For Johann Buddenbrook in Thomas Mann's first novel the chance reading of Schopenhauer is a shattering experience, a fascination of a drug-like nature, irresistible and offering a new form of freedom, freedom from responsibility, freedom to drift to death; his son Hanno's experience of Wagner's music is on similar lines. The far-reaching influence of Freud on the twentieth-century novel takes its origins in the Vienna of the *fin de siècle*, in the anti-rationalism of Nietzsche and in many stimuli from earlier Romantic literature. Since the Neo-Romantic movement in Austria and Germany at the turn of the century the novelist's world has been less tightly confined within the bounds of everyday, common-sense realism. The use of leitmotifs, of symbolism and of myth, and the novelist's scepticism about the inevitable necessity of an ordered sequence of events in time, the breaking-down of man's coherent purpose into a stream of consciousness that consists of a flux of impressions with little more predictability than the random sequence of a pack of cards: this form of the analytical novel, closer often to lyrical poetry than to epic prose, is Romantic in its affinities, and of international tendency, not confined in the least to German literature. The experimental novel of the nineteen-twenties can be seen as a form of Neo-Romantic literature, a desire to widen the confines of the three-dimensional world of most nineteenth-century novelists. James Joyce's *Ulysses*, Proust's *A la recherche du temps perdu*, Kafka's *Das Schloß* ('The Castle') and later the novels of Faulkner are much more significant than the rambling novels of the German Romantics, but fundamentally of the same impulse —analytic, introspective, blurring the edges of the seen world by reference to other dimensions. There is no desire here to avoid seeing the world around, but the urge to see more than was visible to the naked eye of the nineteenth-century realist; a photograph alone is not enough; an X-ray is asked for as well. Virginia Woolf's criticism of Bennett, Wells and Galsworthy was in the cause of liberation from a social realism which was seen as imprisoning to the imaginative mind, and her well-known words of 1919 are relevant in this context:

Examine for a moment an ordinary mind on an ordinary day. The mind receives a myriad impressions—trivial, fantastic, evanescent, or ingraved with the sharpness of steel. From all sides they come, an incessant shower of innumerable atoms, and as they fall, as they shape themselves into the life of Monday or Tuesday, the accent falls differently from of old; the moment of importance came not here but there; so that, if the writer were a free man and not a slave, if he could write what he chose, not what he must, if he could base his work upon his own feeling and not upon convention, there would be no plot, no comedy, no tragedy, and no love-interest or catastrophe in the accepted style . . . Life is not a series of gig-lamps symmetrically arranged; life is a luminous halo, a semi-transparent envelope surrounding us from the beginning of consciousness to the end. Is it not the task of the novelist to convey this varying, this unknown and uncircumscribed spirit, whatever aberration or complexity it may display?

The German Neo-Romantics, the French Symbolists, and the experimental novelists of the nineteen-twenties and after would no doubt contend that their method was an extension and a heightening of the concept of realism in the novel. A causally connected narrative confining itself to events and people that would be generally accepted as plausible in life as a whole—the nineteenth-century realistic novel—is for many contemporary authors no longer an adequate vehicle for expressing their vision. The old classical rules for the playwright embodied a rough-and-ready realism; action must take place within one room and within twenty-four hours; if it does not do this, it cannot claim to be 'realistic', and no audience can be expected to waste time watching it. The twentieth-century novel has sought in a roughly analogous way to extend the bounds of reality as practised by the novelist beyond the confines of the rational common-sense world.

It may be that this attempt at experimentation has been only of limited success; the imposition of an X-ray upon an ordinary photograph hardly provides a clear picture, nor does the X-ray alone reveal what we see on a photograph. But the German novel goes into the non-rational, indeed the supernatural, more easily and more naturally than the French or English novel. For better or for worse, this tendency is present in German writing, more strongly marked in the twentieth century and the Classical-Romantic period than in the main part of the nineteenth century. The result is literature that is less directly entertaining, more introspective and often possessing a more highly wrought prose style than is usual in the novel of social realism.

Rilke's *Malte Laurids Brigge* (1910) will illustrate the point that has just been made, and as an example of a Neo-Romantic novel it offers interesting gradations from detailed realism, through borderland states of mind where the rational world breaks down, to episodes which appear as a sheer negation of the commonsense world. The twenty-eight-year-old Malte, living alone in a seedy district in Paris, records his impressions of the present and his memories of his lonely, anxiety-ridden childhood in Denmark. Malte, like Rilke when he was Rodin's secretary and engaged upon the *Neue Gedichte* ('New Poems'), is attempting, desperately in all conscience, to 'learn to see'. At times he almost manages to compel himself to depict the industrial scene around him with the photographic accuracy of the Naturalist.

That I can't give up sleeping with the window open. Trams tear clanging through my room. Cars go over me. A door shuts. Somewhere or other a pane of glass clatters down, I hear its big pieces laugh and the little splinters giggle. Then suddenly muffled, enclosed noise from the other side, inside the house. Somebody is climbing the stairs. Coming, coming incessantly. Is here, has been here a long time, has gone past. And then the street again. A girl crows out: *Ah tais-toi, je ne veux plus.* The tram races up to this with excitement, rushes over it, away over everything. Somebody calls. People run, overtake one another. A dog barks. What a relief: a dog. Towards morning there is even a cock that crows, and that is unbounded pleasure. Then I suddenly go to sleep.

This is not objective description, but a relating of what is heard to oneself. Malte does not hear the trams and motor-cars, he feels them violating his privacy as a corporeal presence and shock. There is a mass of impressions of things directly experienced, sensations from the outside world, but they are absorbed and given back to paper and print transformed by a poet's imagination.

Realism soon yields to surrealism, an awareness of different and disparate layers of experience simultaneously. Malte sees a poor woman in the street, lost in her private and clearly anxious preoccupations:

The woman started and took herself out of herself, too quickly, too violently, so that her face remained in her two hands. I could see it lying there, its hollow shape. It cost me an indescribable effort to keep my attention on these hands and not to turn to look at what had torn itself away from them. I shuddered at the thought of seeing a face from the inside, but I was even more afraid of the bare, wounded, faceless head.

A passing mental split is described in terms of stark physical violence. For the child Malte these fantasies used to assume more terrifying proportions. Groping for a pencil which he has dropped on to the carpet, he feels his hand to be something alien and uncontrollable; when a second strange hand comes from out of the wall, it is only with terror and difficulty that he can withdraw his own hand. He dresses up in front of a mirror, but becomes horrified at the grotesque figure staring back at him, and ascribes a daemonic power to the mirror; reflection and illusion threaten to become stronger than reality and to engulf him. The psychological realism of these experiences is expressed in terms of subjective illusion bordering close to fantasy; Malte is here poised on a high pinnacle and left balanced precariously on a mere vestige of the everyday world which is open to a nightmare drop into the unknown. When the supernatural intervenes, Malte can accept it without question as part of objective reality. After all, he is not alone in seeing the ghosts of Christine Brahe and Ingeborg.

Rilke's novel, an odd, unique, highly stylized and curiously impressive piece of prose, may then be taken as an example of the fragmentation of the outside world in the poet's experience. Kafka knows how to blend fantasy with realism with equal if not greater skill. He already takes for granted that the lower middle-class environment of pre-1914 Prague will merge at any time from its everyday humdrum tedium into a nightmare world. In his early *Beschreibung eines Kampfes* ('Description of a Fight') he is concerned already with the instability of the common-sense world:

Do you know why I pray like that? . . . Now at last I can reveal to you why I have let myself be accosted by you. From curiosity, from hope. Your look has already comforted me a long time. And I hope to learn from you what it is about the things which sink around me like a fall of snow, while for other people even a little liqueur glass stands firm on the table like a monument.

The predicament of Thomas Mann, Rilke, Kafka and other sensitive writers of the early twentieth century has become more widely shared in the forty or fifty years that have since passed, though seldom more cogently expressed. Two world wars and their aftermath, and the hectic rapidity of the changes in the surface of civilized living everywhere have made even the least percipient of us aware that material things can change and disappear like a fall of snow. The portrayer of contemporary society cannot, and would seldom wish to, depict it in terms of the stability which is so reassuring when we read the work of the nineteenth-century realists. No doubt these earlier novelists were well aware of the transience of the state of things they described; Gotthelf, Keller, Raabe and Fontane certainly were. But for them, whatever their views on ultimate purpose might be, there was a close relation to an existing society, a conviction that people could and should live communally for their mutual well-being. Of the major German prose writers of that period, Conrad Ferdinand Meyer was perhaps the only one who lacked such serenity and had to hold his imaginative world together by bold-seeming gestures. It is very difficult for a serious present-day writer to tell a story in the manner of the three-dimensional realism of the last century without taking into account, at least implicitly, the technical innovations or the probings of the narrative analyst beyond the confines of common-sense externality.

The transition from realism to Neo-Romanticism at the turn of the century was indicative of a new complexity that has come into the twentith-century novel. The more pronounced self-consciousness of the novelist in face of his material is an indication of this. For those who were influenced by Nietzsche the aesthetic approach could now be much more easily divorced from the ethical. If there was no ultimate meaning in religious terms, as there had been with Gotthelf and Stifter, or on the basis of a humanism which assumed that relations between human beings made sense, as was the case with Raabe and Fontane, it was assumed by some that meaning could be found, for a short time at least, in minute preoccupation with patterns of style and an aesthetic and clinical aloofness. The nineteenth-century novel and *Novelle* had been on the whole a purveyor of moral values. Aimed at a wide, middle-class audience, it did well to be didactic and acceptable for family reading. Goethe's *Werther*, an early forerunner of the solitary introspectiveness of Rilke's *Malte Laurids Brigge*, had a general effect on the public which its author subsequently regretted. His two later novels made good what was regarded by many as an irresponsible attitude; *Die Wahlverwandtschaften* discusses marriage and divorce on lines of an orthodox nature, while Wilhelm Meister, in the *Wanderjahre* ('Wilhelm Meister's Years of Travel'), ultimately finds his vocation in specialized work as a surgeon in the service of the community. The tradition of the *Bildungsroman*, the novel of individual development which became the typical longer narrative genre in Germany after Goethe's *Wilhelm Meister*, was firmly didactic; the hero's growth to maturity is followed as an educative process that will improve him and fit him for use in society. With the *fin de siècle* this certainty was lost. Mann's *Buddenbrooks* takes as its theme the decline of a family, as does Rilke's *Malte Laurids Brigge*. Mann's early stories illustrate richly and with many variations the problem of the intelligent man who cannot find a secure relationship to society. He is an artist because he no longer believes in moral purpose nor in the value of the society he lives in; his sharply aesthetic, observer's approach is a substitute for real meaning, but known to be only a substitute, and a sterile one at that. Tonio Kröger regrets the loss of spontaneity which is the fate of the modern aesthete:

Feeling, warm, heart-felt feeling, is always banal and unusable, and the only artistic qualities are the tensions and cold ecstasies of our degenerate, speciously artistic nervous system ... The gift for style, form and expression already takes for granted this cool and pernickety relationship to what is human, yes, takes for granted a certain human impoverishment and desolation . . . The artist is finished as soon as he becomes human and begins to have feelings.

Tonio admittedly refuses to follow the implications of this attitude; he decides tentatively and wistfully to esteem loving kindness, in spite of his coldness and aloofness from ordinary life. Other central figures of Mann's writing in the first decade of the present century illustrate this attitude equally clearly, if not more so: Detlev Spinell in *Tristan*, or Gustav Aschenbach in *Der Tod in Venedig* ('Death in Venice'), for instance.

An early short story by Hugo von Hofmannsthal, 'Reiter-geschichte' ('Cavalry Story', 1899), indicates tellingly the equivocal ambivalence of an attitude such as that of Mann's early heroes when it is transferred from the rarefied level of the professional intellectual to a less esoteric sphere. Told with skill and word-artistry, this brief narrative deploys as its themes a lust devoid of higher feelings, a consciousness of looseness, sordidness and incipient anarchy (a squadron of Austrian cavalry are in skirmishing action in Northern Italy in 1848) and an inexplicable premonition of death; day-to-day living, the background of the nineteenth-century realists, has become temporarily abnormal, traditional morality is lacking, and the story culminates in a brutal and gratuitous murder. If the introspective and refined figures of Mann's early work adopt the cult of art as the only substitute they can find for ethical or religious purpose, the less cultured characters in Hofmannsthal's short story have only an animal violence to fall back upon when conventional sanctions are withdrawn. The experience of meaninglessness finds expression in aesthetic aloofness on one level or in barbarism on another. The sensitivity towards experiences that cannot be contained within the common-sense world is divorced from religion and played with as if it were a pretty toy. Hofmannsthal was acutely aware of this problem, and indeed many authors, earlier and later, have been conscious of the difficulty of reconciling the longings of the artist for colour, vitality and the full exploitation of the senses, with the requirements of social or religious obligation. His novel fragment *Andreas, oder Die Vereinigten* ('Andreas, or the United Ones') was to have been a *Bildungsroman* showing the growth to maturity of a young Austrian who is tempted by a sensual and dishonest servant and subsequently by the quicksilver slipperiness of the people who influence him during his stay in Venice. The later dramas, in particular *Der Turm* ('The Tower'), make clear how hard Hofmannsthal spent himself in the effort to overcome the allurement of the meaningless flux which much of his early work presupposes, and how he rediscovered in a tremendous effort of will-power a doctrine of social responsibility.

Writing on 'William Blake's Visions' Kathleen Raine has said:

> One might say that in this century interest has moved from the Victorian's almost exclusive preoccupation, in art and science alike, with natural appearances to a study of the subjective world . . . Vision, we are able to understand, may express an order as real, if not as tangible, as physical phenomena.

This subjective, visionary quality is, we have maintained, characteristic of a considerable amount of German fiction of our time. Without the binding force of nineteenth-century realism and social consciousness, the novel became open to fragmentation through visionary perception, and at the same time exposed to that revaluation of all values which so frequently led to nihilistic amorality. Paul Ernst's many short stories are overshadowed by this uneasiness, to which he seldom gives an unequivocal answer. In the nineteen-thirties a hectic and distorted form of nationalism imposed a ban on serious exploration of the novelist's major concerns: the critical portrayal of society through the eyes of the imaginative artist, and the free pursuit of a vision of reality and purpose.

The Expressionism of the period just before and after the first world war was an ecstatic radicalism which strove to combine visionary awareness with practical social purpose. Historically this movement has been associated primarily with the drama, while in the field of fiction there is, at the periphery of the movement, one outstanding figure, Franz Kafka, who in European significance has dwarfed all others who are associated with Expressionism. It is through his sketches, stories and three novels that post-war German readers and writers have frequently made their own discovery of symbolism in the novel, of the merging of conscious mind and dream-world, of motifs of fear, guilt and split personality, as also of the sense of metaphysical quest. Kafka has been interpreted in terms of religious seeking; of abnormal psychology with a Freudian basis; of social-political consciousness; or of a deliberate nihilism which expounds life as a hell guided, if there is any guidance at all, by a malevolent fiend. Then there is the thought that Kafka may be a parodist, more subtle than Thomas Mann, who has deliberately constructed stories that shall be open and capable of explanation in terms of any or all of such solutions; the purpose of each work, according to this theory, would be to puzzle and entertain the reader by presenting problems which are capable of various solutions, any one of which may be as valid as another. But the anguish and intense spirit of seeking that pervades his work, though so frequently accompanied by irony and humour of a sort, testifies to its sincerity. The evidence of his intimate friend Max Brod too cannot be dismissed lightly. It may be that Kafka asked for his manuscripts to be destroyed because he felt they would give an equivocal and depressing impression of his aims, and because he saw little use in leaving works to posterity which, he now believed, failed to express what he wanted to say. Kafka's world is fantastic, but his description of it is ordered with great precision; this world is original in a way that few other imaginative worlds invented by authors are. "I am an end or beginning."

Kafka is sceptical about the likelihood of the artist being granted significant status in society, as the two short stories 'Josefine die Sängerin' ('Josephine the Singer') and 'Ein Hungerkünstler' ('A Starvation Artist') show. Josefine sees herself as the inspiring songster of the whole mouse people, but when she requests to be exempt from the normal duties of the mouse-state on the strength of her reputation as an artist, she receives little sympathy. Her fame is short-lived: 'She is a small episode in the eternal history of our people, and the people will get over the loss.' For Kafka all sensitive people, whether they are performers or artists or not, are in need of help and sympathy, for it is the lot of humanity to suffer and their duty to help. The starvation-artist is mono-maniacal too, and in time forgotten. Unlike Josefine the mouse, this man's motives in becoming a virtuoso are not vanity or ambition, but idealism. He is a seeker, discontented with earthly food, and his fasting is an expression of spiritual seeking. The young panther embodies the brutish vitality and thoughtlessness which alone can be integrated in life within the earthly cage. If Kafka's work is pessimistic with regard to the values of normal, material-istic society, its criticism implies a hunger for justice, truth and love which is a conviction of their necessity. The major novel *Das Schloß* has been variously interpreted, but its concern with the nature of religious experience and with the relevance of this experience to man's place in the community around him is evident. The fundamental, unsolved question in the interpretation of Kafka seems to be: Did he believe that his search for meta-physical assurance had been fulfilled or was capable of being fulfilled? In his stories and novels we find no reference to con-temporary events, nor to the history of civilization, and no encyclopaedic recounting of learned facts such as Thomas Mann indulged in. Kafka is concerned with the bare bones of human experience. His careful, studied and unassuming prose is a deceptively simple-looking vehicle for the complexity of his thoughts. He expresses the probings and anxieties of the human mind stretching out to utmost reaches, leaving common sense behind and venturing over the border into the irrational. The subjective seekings and fears of Kafka's mind have now become compelling to general human attention.

II

DOCUMENTATION

IT is likely that the most significant German prose literature of the decade after 1945 will be that which wrestles with the problems of the novel form after the breakdown of nineteenth-century realism and sees them in the context of a struggle for meaning and hope in face of the enervating tendencies of the Neo-Romanticism of fifty years ago. The sombre background of German history in the last twenty-five years has acted as a further challenge to the probing imagination. But many authors have been less concerned with the delineation of a psychological or metaphysical *Ultima Thule* than with the description of German people caught up in a flux of external events. The methods of photographic naturalism, or of a simpler descriptive realism, have on the whole sufficed these writers as a vehicle for conveying their impression of the world of their time. Originality of style, narrative method or conception of human nature count for less in such works than documentary or topical interest. These are books where purely literary merit is in some cases inferior to their attractiveness to the social historian who is looking for the imaginative portrayal of public events. Here the *roman fleuve* comes into its own, where characters tend so easily to become demoted into puppets who must be jerked across a vast backcloth of historical factuality. The social-historical novel quickly loses its topicality, and already with some novels that have appeared in Germany during the last twelve years, the reader has the sense of staleness that comes upon him if he turns over the files of old newspapers in a reference library. Not with all such works, it must be added. A novel which is predominantly of interest because of the picture it gives of German life in our time is hardly likely to be remembered as a literary masterpiece once the topical novelty has worn off; but its extravert qualities and its usefulness as a document should assure it some place in the memory of future students of literature.

Some older authors have an inclination to reconstruct the time of their youth, sometimes because the earlier period shows itself in a more settled perspective than the immediate past and because the pre-1914 era in particular takes on the aura of a golden age; at other times this period is regarded satirically. The chaos of the present is something that goes back further than 1933, and the confusion of values became patent already in 1918; if the seeds of decay were evident already before the first world war, they were visible only to the few, and Europe as a whole took peace and plenty for granted. Max René Hesse (1885–1952), who began publishing fiction in 1930, was concerned with the portrayal of pre-1914 society in his major work, the *Dietrich Kattenburg* trilogy. Hesse was an aloof and elusive figure, independent of literary and political fashions, living for much of his life in South America. The development of his hero Dietrich as a boy and a young man against the social background of his industrialist and officer family in the Lower Rhine area is probably autobiographical. With his high intelligence and his imaginative but unpredictably obstinate temperament, the hero has continued difficulties in adjusting himself to the requirements of society as represented by his upper middle-class family and by the things they value—money, career, pleasure and the Prussian military tradition. This is a solid, straightforward novel, distinguished by its rounded characterization and by its objective realism. The author stands away from his personages and their background, but portrays them with intimate knowledge and unsparing acuity. The folly, intolerance, careless arrogance, hardness and restlessness of these people are not condemned, but demonstrated in their actions; yet for all their faults, these characters lived in an age of security and of generally accepted loyalties, when the pattern of living was more rigid and thus simpler than in later times. With its emphasis on the emergence of the hero's character—Dietrich is introduced to us as a small boy, and leaves us after he has just completed his university course and is about to become a cavalry officer—this work is a *Bildungsroman*; the large cast of subsidiary characters also succeeds in coming to life, and the author has deployed his personages and themes with calculated skill.

A very different picture of pre-1914 society is drawn by Johannes R. Becher in his novel *Abschied* ('Parting', 1948), sub-titled 'a German tragedy: 1900–1914'. Becher, who was born in 1891, has been an active supporter of revolutionary causes from 1918 onwards, and is now one of the most influential literary figures in Eastern Germany. His reputation is firstly as a lyrical poet. Somewhat loosely constructed, this novel remains in the memory as a succession of episodes rather than as a closely knit whole. As a small boy Hans is allowed to stay up to welcome the new year and the new, twentieth century. 'Things must be different'; his grandmother's words are a toast to the new age. But the boy can see no changes at breakfast next morning, and life in this conventional, prosperous home, dominated by an unimaginative, ambitious and irritable father, is strait-laced within narrow, intolerant circumstances. The boy's lively intelligence, combined with an emotionally rooted antagonism to his father's personality, develops into a distrust of all that his father believes in, especially of the noisy glitter of upper-class society. The influence of this environment is shown by Becher as crippling to the development of a humane personality; Hans betrays the poorer boy Hartinger, who has been his friend at the primary school, and shows every sign of becoming a brutalized bully. In adolescence his perplexity and distrust of the values current in society around him bring him into a despairing defiance comparable to that of Dietrich Katten-burg. The solution to this problem, however, is seen in simpler terms by Becher than by Max René Hesse. Hans finds his life's purpose in embracing the cause of revolutionary socialism, and the novel concludes with his refusal to volunteer for military service at the outbreak of the first world war.

Anna Seghers (born 1900) has been well known for a long time as an exponent of the proletarian novel, her most popular work being the war-time *Das siebte Kreuz* ('The Seventh Cross', 1941).

After emigrating to France, and then to Mexico, she returned to live in Eastern Germany after the war. *Transit* (1944) is a complicated story of German refugees desperately seeking means to escape from Marseilles in 1940-1. *Die Toten bleiben jung* ('The Dead Stay Young', 1949) takes a broad canvas and depicts a multiplicity of events and personages. Opening with the revolutionary movement in Berlin in 1918 and concluding with the entry of the Russians in 1945, this work reflects the principal political and social tendencies of the period obliquely through the private lives of the contrasting groups of characters, working-class, peasantry and industrialist and military bourgeoisie. A woman who loses her husband in 1918 and whose only son is killed in action in the Russian campaign of the second world war remains faithful to their Communist cause and is rewarded by the arrival of the Russians in Berlin in 1945. The novel achieves a dramatic climax of some power in the final sections describing the Russian advance westwards. This is a professional and competent piece of writing, comparable to *War and Peace* in its structure, and showing Hitler's invasion of Russia as a repetition of Napoleon's campaign of 1812, though, almost inevitably, falling short of Tolstoy's masterpiece in humanity and wisdom. *Der Ausflug der toten Mädchen* ('The Outing of the Dead Girls', 1947) is the title of a volume of five stories in which Anna Seghers depicts, in black and white terms, the suffering of political resisters to the Nazi régime. The most convincing is 'Die Saboteure' ('The Saboteurs'), which tells of the life of workers in a munitions factory in Mainz during the war. Her three tales, *Die Linie* ('The Line', 1950), published with a birthday greeting to Stalin, are political propaganda rather than literature; the little collection of *Friedensgeschichten* ('Peace Stories', 1950) are more interesting for their reflection of life in Eastern Germany of that period than as literature. These and others of Anna Seghers' shorter tales have been collected in two volumes entitled *Der Bienenstock* ('The Beehive', 1956). Much more satisfactory is the volume of *Kalendergeschichten* (1949), the only volume of short stories by the dramatist Bertolt Brecht (1898-1956). The dry wit of the aphorisms of the 'Stories of Herr Keuner' has been widely appreciated. The tales and verse of this volume, told with a deliberately bare simplicity that is by no means naïve artlessness, consciously hark back to the instructive tone of the early nineteenth-century *Kalender*, or almanacs, which aimed at reaching the widest public.

In addition to Anna Seghers two other novelists may be mentioned who have acquired a considerable reputation in Eastern Germany and who, like her, often treat contemporary themes in the manner of socialist realism. Willi Bredel (born 1902) is the author of a trilogy *Verwandte und Bekannte* ('Relations and Acquaintances', 1943–56) which narrates the fortunes of factory and dock workers in Hamburg in the years before 1914 and the struggles of the next generation to spread their Russo-phile beliefs during the Weimar Republic, while the third volume follows the adventures of Communist resisters to National Socialism. Bodo Uhse (born 1904) has published a semi-auto-biographical novel of an adolescence during the first world war, *Wir Söhne* ('We Sons', 1947), written with freshness of style and feeling. Apart from other prose works, Uhse has written the first volume of a trilogy, *Die Patrioten* ('The Patriots', 1954), dealing with the German-Russian conflict from the point of view of German underground opposition to Hitler.

Arnold Zweig (born 1887), who now also resides in Eastern Germany, wrote his novel *Das Beil von Wandsbek* ('The Axe of Wandsbek', 1947) for the most part during the war years in London. It is an elaboration of a macabre incident reported from Hamburg in 1938. A suburban butcher consents to act as execu-tioner to four political prisoners who are held in Fühlsbüttel prison in order that he may save his business from bankruptcy by earning quick money. Its theme might have made a satirical short story, but scarcely holds the reader's interest when it is expanded into a long novel.

The best remembered book of Alfred Döblin (1878–1957) is *Berlin Alexanderplatz* (1929), which has more than once been compared to Joyce's *Ulysses*. It is, however, a less influential work.

The interior monologue technique is used to express the turgid and confused impulses of its central character, Franz Biberkopf, an East Berlin furniture-removal man, whose sensibilities and intelligence are simpler than those of Stephen Dedalus or Leopold Bloom. Much of the book reflects the animal level of its hero and a preoccupation with the interpretation of experience in terms of scientific materialism. There are poetry and power on occasions, though Biberkopf, imprisoned for the murder of a woman, undergoes after his release from gaol into the strange new world of freedom adventures which are reminiscent of the conventional crime-story. Although this is a novel of experimental interest, its prime hold on the present-day reader is through the plasticity of its evocation of a Berlin working-class milieu through the eyes of a simple, coarse and violent, but pitiable representative of this world. There are few successful German proletarian novels in the tradition of French naturalism, but *Berlin Alexanderplatz* is one of the outstanding ones in this form. During his years of exile from Germany Döblin was working on a tetralogy *November 1918*, which was completed in 1943 and published in Germany after the war. The action of this work is centred on the events of the winter 1918–19, concentrating principally on the stormy days of the revolution in Berlin. Döblin clearly has no regrets for the passing of the old pre-war civilization, and his social sympathies are closer to those of Johannes Becher than Max René Hesse. This novel is a *roman fleuve*, comparable to Jules Romains' *Les hommes de bonne volonté* or John Dos Passos' *U.S.A.* in the attempt to present the wide range of a big city by means of a series of parallel actions which are linked together mainly by the context of their time and place. The hero of Döblin's work is the revolution itself rather than any of the individuals participating in it. The president, Ebert, and the leader of the Freikorps, Noske, are shown in a poor light by comparison with the Spartacist leaders Rosa Luxemburg and Karl Liebknecht, whom the author wishes to vindicate. The narration of these public political events is less satisfying than the action which describes the attempt of an ex-army officer to return to his pre-war occupation as a schoolmaster, his conversion to the Spartacist cause and his subsequent years of anonymous pilgrimage. In spite of many gripping incidents the work is hardly convincing as a whole, and is less compelling than *Berlin Alexanderplatz*.

Edzard Schaper was born in Ostrowo in the province of Posen in 1908, settled in Esthonia in 1930, fled from there to Finland in 1940 and since 1947 has been living in Switzerland. In his novels he looks backward, either to the time when the Baltic lands were under Czarist rule or to the period between the wars when they were independent. One of Schaper's most frequent themes is the suffering of the political prisoner and the need for a schooling in stoicism which he sees as the lot of modern man. This is the message of his two historical novels set in the France of the Napoleonic era (*Die Freiheit der Gefangenen*, 'The Freedom of the Captives', 1949; *Die Macht der Ohnmächtigen*, 'The Power of the Powerless', 1951). In the novel *Die sterbende Kirche* ('The Dying Church', 1935) Schaper describes the struggles of a faithful few to keep alive the Orthodox Christian faith in a little Esthonian town which in the years after 1918 became indifferent, if not hostile, to this community. The devotion and simple humility of Father Seraphim, an old priest, is touchingly portrayed. The dome of the church collapses during the solemn Easter service, causing the death of Father Seraphim and of some members of the congregation; disaster marks the end of this church community's separate existence, and symbolizes too the decay of the Orthodox faith as a whole. *Der letzte Advent* ('The Last Advent', 1949) is a sequel to *Die sterbende Kirche*; it shows the efforts of Sabbas, who has been Father Seraphim's deacon and now feels weighed down with guilt at not having prevented the Easter calamity, to take an active part in extending his church's power. Quixotically he makes an illegal entry into Russia where he works secretly to spread the persecuted faith, only to be captured and to be faced with death. *Der letzte Advent* is a work whose sombreness is unrelieved and whose emotional atmosphere has much in common with the tragedies of the baroque dramatist Gryphius. Immediately attractive, however, is the charming and whimsically sad shorter tale *Die Arche*, *die Schiffbruch erlitt* ('The shipwrecked Ark', 1935), which depicts the disastrous fate of a circus of wild animals that is being shipped from Sweden to Germany.

The experiences and moods of the last war and the most recent past have provided a range of raw material to the realistic novelist which makes the sagas of older authors writing about earlier decades in the century seem unadventurous. The German public has welcomed documentary reporting, satire at the expense of the Third Reich, or testimonies of faith based on personal experience. Apart from work with aspirations to literary value, there have been volume upon volume of autobiography, memoirs, diaries, spy stories, escape stories, medical stories and routine writing in general, poured out to meet the public demand for any novelty claiming to throw light on European conditions in the recent past. The immediacy of this literature of confession, indictment and documentation with regard to the Nazi period has by now probably passed its peak. A negative commitment of protest against National Socialism has remained through nearly all serious novels published in Germany or Austria since the war.

Like Döblin, Kasimir Edschmid (born 1890) is best known as one of the Expressionist *avant-garde*. Soon after the war he brought out a long novel *Das gute Recht* ('One's Proper Right', 1946), which recounts the irritations besetting family life in war-time. An author and his family live during the war in a Bavarian village, where they have an unpleasant family billeted on them. Rotenhan, the author, unable to express himself during the Nazi régime, has devoted himself to writing travel-books; that he should have to share a house with Ziema, a smug and shifty supporter of the powers that be, is a hard blow. This record of the day-to-day difficulties of evacuation has a value as a picture of the time. *Der Zauberfaden* ('The Magic Thread', 1949), another prolix work, follows the vicissitudes of the artificial-silk industry in Wuppertal. Much more convincing than either of the above works is *Wenn es Rosen sind, werden sie blühen* ('If They Are Roses, They Will Flower', 1950). This is a historical novel concerned with the opposition struggles against the Hessian régime in the eighteen-twenties and thirties. The real hero of the book is not Georg Büchner, who takes flight to Strassburg at what transpires to be the expedient moment, but Franz Weidig, the idealistic schoolmaster who stays to face arrest, torture and death.

Hermann Kesten's *Die Zwillinge von Nürnberg* ('The Twins of Nürnberg', 1947) combines comedy with political satire. It follows the chief public events and moods of the two periods described, the two years after the end of the first world war and the years 1938–45. Everything that happens in the complicated but neatly contrived plot is within the bounds of reason, but only just. The twins Primula and Uli get married, the former to an ex-officer who later becomes an official in Goebbels' ministry, the latter to a writer who has to emigrate to Paris because of his humanitarian ideals. Primula becomes the mother of twin boys, both of whom later turn against the Nazi outlook. The later chapters, showing the life of German emigrants in Paris and the conditions in Germany shortly before the outbreak of war in 1939, are more serious in tone than the earlier part of the book. The final chapter which shows the confrontation of Primula, still loyal to the outlook of wartime Germany, with her son Alexander, now a lieutenant in the American army, over the ruins of Nürnberg in 1945, is stark and moving. This novel excels in the skill of its management of plot and situation and in the effectiveness of its dialogue.

Mars im Widder ('Mars in Aries', 1941), by Alexander Lernet-Holenia (born 1897), is interesting less for its love story and the strange private experiences of its hero, an Austrian officer, than for its description of the mobilization of troops in August 1939, the advance of motorized units through Slovakia, the uncertain waiting at the frontier, the invasion on September 1st and the collapse of Polish resistance before the oncoming German forces. The novel closes sixteen days later, when the campaign is over and the Russians are in occupation of Eastern Poland.

The war in Russia has haunted the imaginations of many post-war novelists, though in few cases has the material received outstanding treatment. Willi Heinrich's *Das geduldige Fleisch* ('The

Patient Flesh', English translation 'The Willing Flesh', 1955) is an example of a work which is impressive because of the sheer hugeness and raw vitality of its theme, but in spite of the wealth of observations and experience, this novel remains on a sub-literary level. The material is breath-taking, the action plausible, but the characters thin and novelettish. Erich Landgrebe (born 1908) takes a more limited canvas for his novel of the Russian front. *Mit dem Ende beginnt es* ('It Begins With the End', 1951) relates the experiences of a small group of German soldiers and in particular the relationship of one of them with a young Russian woman. The heroine, on hearing that the man who loved her has been killed, comments: 'I can believe that of him. He was like that. Did not know how to live, but could gladly die.' Heroic nihilism and a fascinated yearning for death are no solution to the problems and confusions of life, Landgrebe tells us. The story is set against the German advance into Russia in 1941, the jaunty mechanized progress in the summer heat and the weary plodding retreat through the grey landscape of snow a couple of years later; the historical events which Plievier was to document so fully are reflected here on a smaller, more subjective scale. Another novel of Landgrebe, *In sieben Tagen* ('In Seven Days', 1955), relates the story of a returned prisoner of war who finds the way back to unity with himself only after a long struggle; his wife and children were killed during the war in an air-raid, but he is helped by two women, a mother and a daughter, to regain confidence to face life.

Kurt Ihlenfeld's *Wintergewitter* ('Winter Thunder', 1951) evokes the atmosphere in a Silesian village in February 1945. The invading army is advancing from the east, and everyone knows that the 'winter thunder' can only be the distant rumbling of guns. In a detailed and quietly realistic exposition the entire village community comes to life. The everyday human problems are overshadowed by foreboding of the unknown—the long-suffered interference of the unpopular régime is about to crumble, but what new terror is to be expected in its place? The central section of the novel consists of the diary of a Lutheran pastor who left

Berlin in September 1944 to take over the care of this village. Deep in the concerns of his heart is the problem of suicide and divine grace; by the Wannsee he visits the grave of the dramatist Kleist and that of a younger man than himself, a gifted poet of the Lutheran faith who together with his family took his life in 1942; the novel contains quotations from the poetry of Jochen Klepper, and is dedicated in part to his memory. The work moves slowly and at times laboriously, but the whole is convincing. We are not presented with any obvious catastrophe. At the end we are still anxiously waiting in the no man's land of a village where all but a handful of the inhabitants have left to trek westwards and where the Russians' entry is to be expected from one day to the next. There is nothing complacent in the author's acceptance of the Christian faith; with much heart-searching he adumbrates the failings of its servants. His central character, the pastor, ruefully notes: 'The safe stronghold has changed into a comfortable house.' Ihlenfeld's second novel, *Kommt wieder, Menschenkinder* ('Come Back, Children of Man', 1954), also a long work, is less convincingly sustained than *Wintergewitter*. Its setting is a working-class district in the French sector of Berlin, close to the zonal boundary in the north. There are the dark tenements, the ruined churches, the lively shops and streets and the primary school by the overhead railway. The action takes place between Ascension and Whitsunday of 1951. A boy of nine meets death when a sudden subsidence of the paved surface causes this unexpected accident. A journalist who has had to face many dangers during the war and as a prisoner of war in Russian hands afterwards feels moved by the fate of this child to raise in his own mind and to discuss with others the religious and philosophical implications of the presence of suffering and evil in the world of a good Creator.

Gerhart Pohl (born 1902) has written in the volume *Wieviel Mörder gibt es?* ('How Many Murderers Are There?', 1953) short stories with an underlying faith in the spirit of truthfulness and love which Ihlenfeld advocates. It was Pohl who was with Gerhart Hauptmann in the last days before the lonely death of the aged dramatist in 1946. A number of these stories portray the relationship between Poles and Germans in the Silesian border-country. They are documents of poignant, unrelieved sadness, starkly realistic in their description of the confusions and ugliness of the war years in this part of Europe, yet sustained (as in the tale 'Engelsmasken', 'Angels' Masks') by an ultimate faith in spiritual values.

Weißt du warum ('Do you Know Why?', English translation 'Vain Glory', 1952), by Dieter Meichsner (born 1928), tells of a senseless attack against the American occupation troops in May 1945 by a band of German resisters who are lurking in the Bavarian Alps. The confusion and cruelty of the situation as it affects the adolescent mind are the emotional basis of the novel. It owes a lot to Hemingway; one thinks in particular of *A Farewell to Arms*; the precarious idyll of innocent love, the beauty of the mountains in spring makes more bitter the revulsion against the condition of the twentieth-century nomadic man of action. There is much that is crude and immature in this novel, but it has vigour. The author's energies have been over-diffused in his second novel *Die Studenten von Berlin* ('The Students of Berlin', 1954), which brings too many personages together under the central cover of the fate of Berlin in the last days of the war and its position as a beleaguered garrison during the time of the airlift. The life of the battered and divided city is reflected in particular through the student community of the Free University established in Berlin after the war.

Hans Werner Richter (born 1908) is sober and disillusioned in his realism. He has a professional accomplishment that seems to be the type of writing that Meichsner is aiming at in a more uncertain manner. Richter's confident manner is already evident in his first novel *Die Geschlagenen* ('The Defeated', 1949), a documentary story of defeat and imprisonment. *Sie fielen aus Gottes Hand* ('They Fell Out Of God's Hand', 1951) is a large-scale novel which recounts the adventures of a dozen characters from the eve of the invasion of Poland, September 1939, to a day in 1950 when they are all collected in a camp for displaced persons in Germany.

None of these figures is German by birth—there are men and women from the Baltic lands, Poland and Russia, from the Balkans, from Luxemburg, France or Spain—but all of them are bound up in their separate way with the fate of Germany. The author seldom commits himself to comment on their fortunes; he prefers to report, and we are told that the material for his characters and plots was based on a factual investigation of individual cases. His sympathies are with the helpless individual, of whatever nationality he may be, who is exposed to the bewildering, incalculable chances of war and its subsequent confusion. Richter handles his large cast with skill, and sketches in the rapidly changing scenes with adroitness, for we are not limited to Central Europe, but are transported to America, Africa, Israel and Vietnam. The net is cast widely, and it is not surprising that the deeper aspects of human experience elude the author. Richter employs a similar method in the novel *Du sollst nicht töten* ('Thou Shalt Not Kill', 1955). The ground covered is the war, from its outbreak to its finish, and the episodes are located far and wide throughout Europe. What unity there is in this panorama is provided by family ties. Carelessness of style and construction and a certain crudity of approach to erotic subject-matter detract from Richter's power as a novelist.

Luise Rinser (born 1911) likes to take a strong woman-character, usually of a forceful kind, and to build her novels round such a central figure. *Mitte des Lebens* ('Middle of Life', 1950) is a love-story that has something of the fire and careless vitality of D. H. Lawrence. The heroine here has taken part in the underground movement against the Nazi régime, has been imprisoned, has achieved some success as a writer after 1945, and, as we take leave of her, is on her way to take up work with an English family. But these events are only peripheral to a character whose mainspring of being lies in her passionate and unhappy sex-life. Her portrait is shown to us largely through the eyes of an older man who has loved her long and intensely. The novel has underlying tenderness and pity which are its most endearing qualities. *Daniela* (1953) centres upon a young woman who feels impelled to leave her comfortable middle-class home background in order to take up practical social work in a forlorn and poverty-stricken community whose living depends on the peat from the moorlands. The story of Daniela's rehabilitation of these people forms the major part of the narrative. The heroine's relationship with the village priest occasions a far-fetched conclusion to the novel which is hardly consistent with what has gone before. *Der Sündenbock* ('The Scapegoat', 1955) is about crime, malice and the murder of a wicked great-aunt by a young woman whose motives the reader is expected to regard sympathetically. The psychological situation is complex rather than convincing. The shorter tale *Jan Lobel aus Warschau* ('Jan Lobel from Warsaw', 1948) is quietly told and effective in its tension and atmosphere. The arrival of a homeless and hunted Polish Jew in an Upper Bavarian village shortly before the end of the war brings problems of an emotional character to the market-gardening household which gives him refuge. Luise Rinser's writing is concerned primarily with personal relationships, and it often shows an acute awareness of emotional reality from a woman's point of view.

Rudolf Krämer-Badoni (born 1913) became known with his satirical novel *In der großen Drift* ('In the Big Drift', 1949), which remains his most interesting work. It is the autobiography of a man who begins in an obscure way in the early nineteen-thirties, is buffeted about by circumstances and ideas in his student days, finds himself in the army without quite knowing how he got there, becomes a war-hero in Russia and is presented to Hitler, again without any ambition on his own part for such distinction, and when it is all over finds himself clearing bomb-damage from the streets of Frankfurt. This book is no novel of individual development, for in its formal models it goes back to the earlier picaresque type of fiction. His hero is the little man who takes things as he finds them, whose first aim in life is to get by, bitterly sceptical as he is of all pretentiousness and sentimentality. *Der arme Reinhold* ('Poor Reinhold', 1951) has a more lyrical, contemplative touch. Reinhold, nearly sixty, lives as a wood-cutter in a rough shed in the Rhine area and recounts the story of his life; from his lower middle-class home life in Frank-furt he goes to the Church, but in the nineteen-thirties his un-orthodox behaviour compels him to leave the order, and since then he has been living as an otherworldly pilgrim, taking no thought for the morrow and doing good works as and when the opportunities offer. *Die Insel hinter dem Vorhang* ('The Island Behind the Curtain', 1955) is a political satire on the well-worn theme of the naïve Russian who comes out West and is bewildered by what he sees.

The need of younger, and older, writers to treat the happenings of the immediate past in fictional form is already clear from the selection, and it is only a selection, of novels that have been discussed above. It is as well to remind ourselves that the reading public, in its demand for writing on these themes, does not necessarily turn first to the writers with serious literary aspirations, but to authors who provide more sensational fare. Erich Maria Remarque (born 1898) wrote with *Im Westen nichts Neues* ('All Quiet On the Western Front', 1929) the most successful popular novel about the first world war, and his *Arc de Triomphe* (1946), the story of a German refugee surgeon in Paris just before the last war, has been a best-seller too; he has continued to write more recently on similar lines. Hans Hellmut Kirst's *Null-acht-fünfzehn* ('Zero Eight Fifteen', 1954–5) has had a quick success, compar-able to that of Remarque's fiction, as a best-selling treatment of topical material. The first volume, describing German barracks life under Hitler in the thirties, is the most lively of the trilogy; the satire on the brutality of a sergeant-major's discipline and the way in which one of the men brings about his discomfiture are effective, though the characters are little more than caricatures. The humour is undeniably there, but it is not often subtle.

Theodor Plievier (1892–1955) completed shortly before his death a trilogy which is a large-scale epic of the war between Germany and Russia and its aftermath. His manner of composi-tion is hardly fiction in the normal sense, for there is so much emphasis on documentation and the narration of tactical move-ments that few of the many characters receive individual treatment. This is particularly the case with the first two volumes of the work. *Stalingrad* (1946) surveys the events leading to the defeat of the Germans in Stalingrad in January 1943. Its sequel *Moskau* (1952) takes as its starting-point the first days of the German invasion of Russia in June 1941, and culminates in the approach of the fateful Russian winter as the Germans stand before Moscow. Plievier had unique facilities for collecting the material for this work; as a refugee from Germany in 1933, he made his way to Russia, and was allowed to observe the scene and to sift the documents of this piece of recent history. The events of the war in the east are told as a vivid and detailed piece of reporting in the naturalist manner. The impetus behind Plievier's writing turns from political theory to a more universal sympathy and pity. In *Moskau* a German whose life has been spared by Russian partisans reflects:

'Germans and Russians lay frozen in the snow.
'What had they wanted? What had their rulers intended with them? They wanted to decide the fate of Europe. Not for the first time . . . Charles XII was ruined on the fields of Poltava. The French musketeers of Napoleon failed. The German grenadiers now lay on the same frozen earth. Europe remained unborn, and the peoples on either side of the bloody wound are suffering hopelessly . . .'

The words of an old Russian man offer prophetic meaning to the despairing German:

'The earth has been given to men from God's hands without any frontiers . . . The whole earth belongs to all, entirely!'

Berlin (1954), the longest of the three parts of the work, brings the novel to its conclusion. As an imaginative work it is the most satisfactory part of the whole, for Plievier brings to life the city of Berlin and the surrounding Eastern Zone with a vigour and variety of treatment that make fascinating reading. Plievier himself came back to Berlin in 1945 with the Russians, and was in a responsible position as a cultural official in the Democratic Republic until 1947, when he fled from the East as a refugee to Western Germany. There is much that must be autobiographical in this novel which traces the fortunes of Berlin from the last days of Hitler in April 1945 through the early days of Russian occupation until it concludes with the abortive rising of June 1953. Most impressive is the picture of Berlin burning while Hitler, now a bleary and fanatical phantom-demon, was still giving his orders from his bunker, that kingdom on which the sun never rose. The city is a comet fallen still blazing from the firmament, a witches' sabbath on the Brocken, a jungle of smoke and burning ash, a Wagnerian twilight of the gods. Plievier's descriptions here are poetic and passionate, as well as detailed and documented. The latter part of the book, which shows for the most part the struggles of a politician who tries to administer just government in the Eastern Zone and the life of German prisoners of war in Russian hands, deflects the author's virulence from Hitlerism to the Communist order. A work which began under the auspices of Russian patronage ends as an uninhibited condemnation of the Russian occupation of Eastern Germany. Indeed, the march of events can play wry tricks on a writer who takes his time in compiling a long-term documentary novel.

III

PAST TIME

WERNER BERGENGRUEN (born 1892) puts a conscious stress on action and dramatic construction in his work, increasingly so as his work has progressed. *Das große Alkahest* ('The Great Alkahest', 1926), which belongs to a whole group of historical novels written in the nineteen-twenties, is not as yet written in the incisive, economic style of the author's later work, but it contains themes which recur constantly there. The incompatibility of true religion with worldly power and the constant tension between ruler and ruled are brought out in the relationship of the arbitrary father von Karp and his timid and irresponsible son who leaves Poland for St. Petersburg. *Der Großtyrann und das Gericht* ('The Tyrant and Judgment', English translation 'A Matter of Conscience', 1935), deservedly one of the most read novels of its time in Germany, brings out Bergengruen's concern for morality and justice in a rigorously dramatic manner; psychological analysis and descriptive atmosphere are reduced to a minimum, so that the action may be revealed in a series of conversations; the culprit, who is ruler of a small Italian Renaissance state, exposes by his action the demoralizing results of justice based on expediency, not on principle. It is both an allegory and a detective story of great competence. *Am Himmel wie auf Erden* ('On Earth as It is in Heaven', 1940) is a long novel set in Berlin in the early sixteenth century. Although the plot is complex, the whole is convincing, and the historical background is carefully filled in. The main theme is fear; Carion, astrologer to the Elector Joachim, foresees a new Flood of Biblical proportions that shall destroy Berlin. The Elector tries to prevent panic by suppressing the prophecy, while at the same time wishing to act upon it. The flood, of course, does not materialize; but this fear is replaced in Carion's case by a greater terror—the anticipation of leprosy.

It is to be expected that a writer of Bergengruen's gifts should turn to the *Novelle*, and probably such polished short works as *Die drei Falken* ('The Three Falcons', 1937), *Der spanische Rosenstock* ('The Spanish Rose-tree', 1940) and *Das Beichtsiegel* ('The Seal of the Confession', 1946) have been more widely read than the novels. The collection of tales *Der Tod von Reval* ('Death in Reval', 1939) treats the theme of death, but with a macabre humour that is far removed from the seriousness of *Die drei Falken* or *Das Beichtsiegel*. Bergengruen has written a study of E. T. A. Hoffmann, and these tales which look back to the legends and gossip of the Baltic seaboard where the author spent his early years are worthy representatives of the tradition of fantasy and realism peculiar to Hoffmann's work. The volume of short stories, often little more than anecdotes, set in the Italian Renaissance, *Der Sternenstand* ('The Position of the Stars', 1947), is, however, less satisfying; for all the glitter and virtuosity, many of these short *Novellen* are lacking in warmth and humanity.

Bergengruen is an accomplished entertainer in all his many shorter stories, and a fertile fabricator of varied plots. But the ease with which he can tell a story is a temptation, and his post-war writing often lacks emotional depth. *Pelageja* (1947) is a short novel, a tale of shipwreck and adventure in North America in the early nineteenth century. Related by a sailor who has survived the experience, the story is not only simple in its narrative method, but is so straightforward in its approach to the human problem that the reader feels himself in a world of boyhood adventure, and furthermore one that is less complex than that of Robert Louis Stevenson's *Treasure Island*. *Das Feuerzeichen* ('The Beacon', 1949) has as hero a man who recalls Kleist's Michael Kohlhaas; living on the Baltic coast at the beginning of the present century, this man bitterly resents an injustice and the assumed slight on his sense of humour, and finally commits suicide. The novel is close to *Der Großtyrann und das Gericht* in theme, though perhaps less fresh and absorbing. *Der letzte Rittmeister* ('The Last Captain of

Horse', 1952) is a work with an atmosphere all of its own, a quaint exoticism spiced with playful irony. The book is dominated by the mellow personality of an old ex-captain of horse who grew up in the army traditions of Czarist Russia and after 1918 drifted about Europe in resigned and by no means unhappy obscurity until he settled to spend his last years in the Tessine. The author, writing as a friend of his old age, records twenty-four short tales which he has heard from the Rittmeister's lips. Many of these stories tell of knights and cavalry officers of bygone days, especially in nineteenth-century Russia, and their principal theme is to extol codes of chivalry which have disappeared with the advent of mechanized armies and industrial society. Though charming and skilfully told, the stories themselves are slight, and it is the benign figure of the whimsical, slightly melancholy and self-confessedly anachronistic Rittmeister who gives this work its unity. *Die Rittmeisterin* (1954) continues the theme and manner of *Der letzte Rittmeister*, though it rambles around its material with a garrulousness that is surprising in a writer who is such a competent adept at the *Novelle* form. The Rittmeisterin is the muse who can fire a man with poetic dreams. The narrator meets in Geneva Musa Petrowna, who, born in Baltic Russia during the first world war, has been a displaced person virtually all her life. They exchange reminiscences of their mutual friend the late Captain of Horse. If Musa Petrowna cherishes the memory of the Rittmeister, Bergengruen can recall a summer of his boyhood by the Baltic coast which remains in his memory because of his devotion to the simple maidservant Anze. This work is ornamented with playful arabesques and allusions. *Die Flamme im Säulenholz* ('The Flame in the Timber Beam', 1955) is a further collection of *Novellen*, this time without the elaborate framework of *Der letzte Rittmeister*, but again bringing back the author's memories of the Baltic lands, dominated by a nostalgia for earlier times.

Bergengruen is undoubtedly one of the most readable of the important living writers of German fiction, and has produced an impressive quantity of writing over the last thirty years. His best work was produced in the decade 1935–45, at a time when he was often at loggerheads with the Nazi régime; it is to these years that his two most important novels, his best known lyrical poetry and a wealth of good *Novellen* belong. If he avoids the contemporary scene as a setting for his stories, topical issues have sometimes appeared in his work in a disguised shape; above all, ethical problems of truth, justice and love in their relationship to human frailty are his finest inspiration. Much of his fiction takes its formal models from the nineteenth-century tradition of the *Novelle*, and especially are we reminded of the Italian forebears of this form of story-telling in the glittering smoothness with which he shapes and finishes his tales. Bergengruen's attitude to the novelist's craft is cool and professional (indeed his smooth accomplishment can be rather too facile), and his emphasis on dramatic tension is a significant contribution to contemporary German narrative method.

If Bergengruen's most recent writing is disappointing because it has ceased adequately to contend with contemporary issues, this is by no means the case with the work of Germany's foremost woman-novelist, Gertrud von Le Fort. Born in 1878 of a Calvinist family that was on her father's side originally of French origin, it was after her conversion to Catholicism that she began writing, her first verse *Hymnen an die Kirche* ('Hymns to the Church', 1926) being of a directly devotional character. Through her father, who had been an officer in the German army before 1914, she was strongly impressed by the traditional conservatism of that period, and much of her writing shows her consciousness of its attractiveness to her while at the same time she rejects it as inadequate and misleading in favour of an uncompromising religious commitment which, she believes, should suffuse all aspects of human life. Many of her stories have a historical setting, though never for merely decorative purposes, for the conflicts and anguish which form her recurring themes are never absent. In her use of the historical *Novelle* she no doubt owes something to Conrad Ferdinand Meyer and Ricarda Huch. She is aware of the disintegrating forces which threaten the stable world she cherishes, but in face of the destruction of normal society she asserts a resolute faith in transcendental values. This faith governs her attitude to the question of war-guilt which she examines in a short essay 'Unser Weg durch die Nacht' ('Our Way through the Night', 1949). Here she protests against the mass-conception of 'the Germans', insisting that every people remains a collection of individuals, and that Germans were capable both of crimes and of devoted humane helpfulness during the period when normal civilization had broken down. Human weakness, she says, may not be glossed over, but neither may it be condemned out of hand; however questionable and sinful a man's behaviour may have been, it nevertheless remains a Christian's duty to love that man. There is a moral, didactic tone running through all her work which has made it an object of admiration to those who share her faith, and its sincerity and accomplishment have given those who disagree with her outlook little opportunity for negative criticism or satire. Gertrud von Le Fort's world of fiction stands firmly within the limits of her conviction of pre-ordained purpose; it has a framework of inner certainty, though it depicts peoples who have to wrestle hard for the retention of their sanity and faith. Without their metaphysical certainty these characters would be exposed defenceless to the corrupting forces of fear, worldliness and violence.

Her first *Novelle*, *Die Letzte am Schafott* ('The Last at the Scaffold', 1931), shows the fear which overwhelms a young Carmelite nun when she is faced with martyrdom in Paris during the French Revolution. This tale, translated into French by Bernanos, has formed the libretto of an opera by Poulenc. The heroine, whose extreme sensitiveness exposes her to onslaughts of despair and anxiety, has much in common with Rilke's Malte, and for Gertrud von Le Fort's suffering women characters religious faith is the one bulwark against a nightmare world of neuroses, but at the same time it is no easy escape from personal responsibility. *Die magdeburgische Hochzeit* ('The Magdeburg Wedding', 1938) is a dramatically told novel of the resistance of Protestant Magdeburg during the Thirty Years War and her storming by Tilly's Imperialist forces. Violence in the name of religion appears to the author as an evil that is harder to accept as part of the ordering of the world than the conflicts of a later age, when the believer is usually in the simpler position of being the victim of a form of worldliness which he can and must reject. *Das Schweißtuch der Veronika* ('The Sudarium of Veronica', 1928-46) is Gertrud von Le Fort's principal work on a large scale. It is less obviously stylized than *Die magdeburgische Hochzeit*, and is a novel of the development of a young woman. With detailed analysis, though always with a logical clarity of exposition, the heroine's girlhood in pre-1914 Rome is presented, revolving round the problems of faith; Veronika has been brought up outside the Church by her positivist grandmother, but is led to it by her own religious experiences. The second section of the novel takes place in Heidelberg soon after the end of the first world war. Here Veronika becomes engaged to Enzio, who has returned from the war disillusioned and embittered at his country's defeat. The incompatibility of Enzio's violent adherence to Nietzsche's outlook with Veronika's devout Catholicism forms the basic theme of the novel. Veronika, highly strung and impressionable—she is known as 'Spiegelchen' because as a child she was a mirror open to all images and influences from outside—humble, weak and confused, earnest and innocent, embodies the female principle as Gertrud von Le Fort conceives it, as complementary and yet opposed to the male. Enzio, the sceptical and amoral intellectual, has been swayed by the teaching of Nietzsche and the melancholy of the Neo-Romantics; religious scepticism and an artist's hunger for worldliness, combined with a restless hankering after violent action, have led him to an embittered and distorted expression of patriotic sentiment. The teachings of liberal humanism, as represented by the philosophy professor who is Veronika's guardian while she is in Heidelberg, are shown as inadequate in face of the two extremes of ruthless nationalism and religious principle. The conclusion of the novel shows Enzio and Veronika reconciled and prepared for marriage; it would have been a happier ending, certainly a more credible one, if the author had let Veronika take her guardian's advice and make a complete break with the tiresome Enzio. *Das Schweißtuch der Veronika*, by virtue of its closeness to the *Bildungsroman* tradition, unfolds in a broad, leisurely manner, but the sense of dramatic urgency is not lost.

In her *Novellen* Gertrud von Le Fort writes with a formal economy and a burnished dignity which recalls Meyer's work; he too was facinated by the art and traditions of Italy. The volume *Die Tochter Farinatas* ('The Daughter of Farinata', 1950) contains four stories which centre on various aspects of the struggle between worldliness and power-lust on the one hand and the need for resignation and love on the other as the only effective means of subduing the evil in the human heart. Bice, daughter of the dead hero Farinata, saves the city of Florence from destruction in the feuds between Guelph and Ghibelline—but by means of humility and outward defeat.

And now that she had after all again been delivered to him wholly without protection, he became aware with deep emotion that there is nothing more inviolate than the unprotected, nothing holier than the unguarded . . . For the will to destruction of this world shatters only against pity, and against nothing else.

Since the end of the last war, Gertrud von Le Fort has written mainly *Novellen*, more often in a historical setting, but always with a reference to topical or moral problems. In her seventy-seventh year she published the two tales *Gelöschte Kerzen* ('Extinguished Candles', 1953) which bring heart-searching conflicts of the post-war period as a framework to two inset stories referring to the time of the Thirty Years War, and which show as fine a grasp of present-day problems as any writing by younger authors. 'Die Verfemte' ('The Outlawed Woman') recounts how a woman helped a Swedish officer to elude his captors during the Thirty Years War and how her memory was regarded with shame by subsequent generations of her family; her deed, how-ever, is vindicated in the situation of flight from the advancing Russians in 1945. 'Die Unschuldigen' ('The Innocents') is a stark tale of the suffering of children during the last war, with particular reference to the village of Oradour. The narrator is a boy whose mind ultimately snaps, leading to his death, on account of too heavy a burden of fear and responsibility which weigh upon him. The story *Am Tor des Himmels* ('At Heaven's Gate', 1954) follows in its technique the manner of *Gelöschte Kerzen*; the arrest of Galileo by the Inquisition and his recantation of his astronomical discoveries are narrated from an old manuscript by a young doctor to a middle-aged woman as they shelter together in a cellar during an air-raid in Germany. Gertrud von Le Fort discusses the implications of Galileo's new knowledge for religious faith. 'We have no longer a God Who cares for us, we have only ourselves now,' one character deduces from the revelation of the new picture of the universe. 'Can something be contradictory to belief, if it is the truth?' is another question. Galileo's recantation is interpreted as an act, not of fear and trembling, but of ironical defiance; if the Church refuses to face facts, he too will be cynical. The temptation to abuse authority is here pervading and corrupting the Church. The conflict between totalitarian authority and religious principle is for Gertrud von Le Fort more clear-cut in the twentieth century than it was in the time of Galileo. The seventeenth century, with its burning preoccupation with questions of religious belief, in terms of oppression and warfare as well as of piety and mysticism, has long fascinated Gertrud von Le Fort. Galileo's new interpretation of the cosmos is shown as having a significance for the seventeenth century which the discovery of nuclear fission has for our own time. It is interesting to compare this story with Bertolt Brecht's drama *Leben des Galilei* ('Life of Galileo'), which was written during the dramatist's exile from National Socialism after he had read about the splitting of the atom. Brecht makes Galileo recant before the Inquisition through fear of physical pain, and shows in a stark epilogue the tragedy of the scientist's last years. Gertrud von Le Fort is again concerned with unjust persecution for conscience' sake in *Der Turm der Beständigkeit* ('The Tower of Constancy', 1957). In eighteenth-century France, though intellectual life is worldly and sceptical, Huguenots are still incarcerated for their beliefs by a state that is nominally Roman Catholic. A sophisticated courtier is brought up with a shock by immediate experience of what such persecution can mean to human beings. This *Novelle* depends too much on intrigue in its plot, and is therefore less impressive than *Die Frau des Pilatus* ('Pilate's Wife', 1955), a story illuminating the struggle between worldly and spiritual forces in the imagined relationship between Pontius Pilate and his wife when they are confronted by the challenge of Christ. Once more it is the woman who follows the voice of the heart and finds salvation and martyrdom, while her husband persists in his refusal to look towards the light. The narrative and the resultant issues are presented with a simplicity which shows how Gertrud von Le Fort has avoided exposing herself to the charge of not facing the complexities of twentieth-century thought and has yet succeeded in recapturing the directness of an earlier age of story-telling.

IV

THE IDYLLIC IDEAL

ONE strand of writing that has persisted in German literature since the eighteenth century is that which may be called the idyllic. If the *Sturm und Drang* under the leadership of the youthful Goethe developed a cult of vitalism and the superman that anticipated Nietzsche a century later, the poets of the Göttinger Hain preferred domestic realism and an outlook of humble resignation, usually in a bucolic setting. This praise of the simple virtues and an acceptance of day-to-day living in the countryside as the healthy obverse to the sophistication of city life received encouragement from Rousseau's doctrine of the return to nature. Goethe was profoundly aware of the dichotomy within himself of restless striving and quiet acceptance, represented often in his work by the symbols of the wanderer and the cottage, or the eagle and the dove. Jean Paul's novels contain pictures of whimsical characters from small-town or village life whose provincial limitations are intended to appear both as absurd and yet also as natural and good. Heine and the Young Germans of the period of the July Revolution of 1830 distrusted this tendency to self-limitation in a regional setting as a refusal to accept political and social responsibility, and it is true that writers such as Stifter, Mörike or Storm had little sympathy with political commitment as the Young German movement conceived it. Mid-nineteenth-century realism is predominantly of a regional quality, with an acceptance of family life in a peasant or middle-class environment as a condition in which a life of harmonious, almost ideal relationships within an unproblematic community may be achieved. This outlook was regarded by the urban Naturalists and Neo-Romantics as no longer valid in an age when civilization was becoming too complex to be covered by so simple a formula.

Up till today there has been a continued demand for writing which follows the idyllic tradition of the eighteenth and nineteenth centuries, and this field of writing has retained a greater popularity in modern German writing than in contemporary English or French writing. The starker forms of naturalistic description are avoided, the often agonized questioning and self-exposure of the Austrian Neo-Romantics or the Expressionists are replaced by an ideal of harmony derived from a cult of feeling. Stylistically this means frequently an attempt to revive the measured dignity of Goethe's later works and the prose of Stifter. It is a manner that is particularly difficult to practise successfully in the mid-twentieth century, when German, like other languages, has shown itself readily adaptable to the colloquialisms and technologically based style of the modern world. To treat contemporary themes in a manner reminiscent of more than a hundred years ago is to run the risk of being charged with escapism and deliberately putting back the clock.

Hans Carossa (1878–1956) was one of the very few authors who succeeded in the task of producing work of some literary quality that describes the contemporary world in this particular traditional manner. His major work is the sequence of volumes of autobiography which began in 1922 with *Eine Kindheit* ('A Childhood') and concluded with *Der Tag des jungen Arztes* ('The Young Doctor's Day', 1955). The proximity of this undertaking to Goethe's autobiography in approach is evident, as is Carossa's writing as a whole in various ways. This major work of Carossa's is episodic in form, and not fiction. The volume *Ungleiche Welten* ('Unequal Worlds', 1951) is an independent account of its author's experiences during the Nazi régime. 'The German man of letters in the totalitarian state had become a suspect figure', he writes here. 'He was compelled either to be silent or at least to pass over in silence very essential phenomena of the contemporary world. Whichever attitude he assumed, from the non-German point of view he appeared either as provincially limited or as false.'

Carossa notes with disapproval that soon after the end of the war voices could be heard hoping that a third world war between Russia and America and Britain would come about, so that Germany might profit from it; or that the persecution of the Jews would soon be forgotten, or shrugged off as something admittedly terrible, but surely no worse than the cruelties of other nations and periods. Carossa's retrospection upon the Nazi period does not offer simple solutions to political problems, but like Gertrud von Le Fort this author thought in terms of a 'great lifting of the hearts' without which 'no bread grows in the fields. Let each man be reconciled with himself; a time will come when he will be alone with his own soul.' As a pendant to *Ungleiche Welten* Carossa added a tale which gives an impression in narrative form of the summer of 1947. 'Ein Tag im Spätsommer 1947' ('A Day in the Late Summer of 1947') conjures up the abnormally dry summer of that year in a Germany still in a condition of extreme exhaustion after the exceptionally hard winter preceding it. Set in the Bavarian countryside, there is unfolded to us the natural beauty of the landscape and the confusion in people's lives from the point of view of an elderly couple who maintain their serenity in spite of the unusual conditions of life all around them. Although there may be much evil and brutality in the world, the opportunities for acts of loving kindness are multiplied and their value is always the same.

Hermann Hesse (born 1877) is a more prolific writer than Carossa and more varied in his themes and settings, but he has maintained a fluent smoothness of style which makes his writing an effortless pleasure to read, even though he spins out his material rather too finely and his characterization often lacks firmness and bite. His earlier short stories and *Novellen*, as in the volume *Kleine Welt* ('Little World'), are almost wholly in the manner of the regional realists; in this case the district is the countryside of Württemburg and the small town of Calw where the author was born. Whimsical and slightly ironical stories such as 'Ladidel' or 'Die Verlobung' ('The Engagement') are a mild and gentle parallel to Arnold Bennett's work, while elsewhere a lyrical and drifting melancholy, accompanied by a backward looking to the Romanticism of the early nineteenth century, supervenes. Already before the first world war Hesse had made his home in Switzerland, after extensive travels which included a journey to India in 1911. The problematic note became accentuated in his writings after 1914, and his public disavowal of German military policy in that year brought him temporary unpopularity and caused him to examine more critically the existing state of society. Didacticism and the fantasy element now became more evident in his tales, and a growing interest in psycho-analysis, oriental mysticism and also the themes of Expressionism left their mark on his work during the nineteen-twenties. There is a sharper edge to novels such as *Demian* (1919) and *Der Steppenwolf* (1927), where a restless dissatisfaction with the contemporary world does not lead him to support any outward social doctrine, but to re-emphasize what has always been his central theme, his belief in the necessity of an integrated inward life, in what E. M. Forster has called the 'developed heart'. The novel *Narziss und Goldmund* (1930) takes up again the opposition between the lure of a restless, many-faceted artist's life and self-limitation along lines of a concentrated and ascetic intellectualism. Hesse has more than once expressed his opinion on the place of Nietzsche as a thinker of disturbing importance. Hesse himself has throughout his writings also been a rebel against establishment, in particular against the official German point of view which he depicts as imposing itself upon school life and adult society with an efficiency that is deadly to the sensitive, independent poet's spirit.

Hesse's last major work, *Das Glasperlenspiel* ('The Game of Glass Beads', English translation 'Magister Ludi', 1943), is his most important novel. It is set in a future time which has achieved an enviable stability, though even so there are indications that this equable society, with its echoes of the Swiss middle classes, contains the seeds of decay within itself. It is an age which has reacted against the intellectual superficiality and triviality of the 'journalistic age', which includes the two or three centuries extending from the age of enlightenment to the present day.

Apart from the mass of the population there exists the Castilian Order, a quasi-monastic élite which in the game of glass beads pursues a distillation of the essence of higher artistic, academic and religious thought and experience. 'The game of glass beads is thus a game with the entire contents and values of our civilization, it plays with them as a painter, for example, in the great periods of art may have played with the colours of his palette. Whatever insights, lofty thoughts and works of art mankind has produced in its creative periods, whatever subsequent epochs of learned observation have expressed in concepts and have made their intellectual possession, this huge complex of intellectual and spiritual values is played by the glass-beads player as an organ is played by an organist.' The Order is not concerned with analytical reason alone, but seeks to find the binding thread, conceived fleetingly in normal artistic or religious experiences, which enables the game at its best to become 'the quintessence of intellect and art, the sublime cult, the mystic union of all the separate members of the universe of letters'. In this 'sublime alchemy' the dissonances of scepticism are forbidden, and the object in view is always to be the search for harmony. Its development is from intellectual to aesthetic, and thence to religious awareness; from mathematics through music to mysticism. Above all, music is for Hesse the most acceptable symbol for this quest for inner unity. The practice of this cult by the intellectual élite in their academies is to act as a leaven to the society of the outside world. The novel follows the development of one man, adhering closely to the pattern of the traditional *Bildungsroman*. Josef Knecht rises early in his adult life to the position of highest responsibility in the Order, and his inward wrestlings concerning the ultimate justification of this institution's existence are described at length. Although Josef's surname is 'Servant', he becomes in fact a rebel against the discipline of the Order and asserts his individuality by abandoning his office in order to serve humanity as he thinks fit. This is in clear contrast to Wilhelm Meister ('Master') in Goethe's novel, the hero who is shown as gradually forgoing his own freedom of personal life in order to submit to the will of the 'Society of the

Tower'. In spite of his long schooling in Kastalien, Josef Knecht has not found inner harmony, and the restlessness of Hesse's earlier heroes reasserts itself in his spirit. From his old friend Plinio he hears the reproach that the Order has lost contact with normal human problems, and this reproach is confirmed by observation of his collegue Tegularius, whose personality has become over-refined and remote as a result of the Order's discipline. The conclusion of the novel shows the sudden collapse of Josef's plans for going out into the world and acting as mediator between it and the Castilian Order. His death by drowning, when swimming in an Alpine lake with the youth to whom he is to act as tutor, appears as a fortuitous catastrophe, though we are to assume that his demise has not been in vain, since it will act as a lasting inspiration to his pupil. Hesse's novel is effective through its discussions and the idealistic spirit which pervades it, but it suffers through loose construction and thinness of characterization. The author mentions in the course of his narrative that he is writing about an age that regards 'personality', individual separateness, as something pathological; but this does not make it easier for the twentieth-century reader to feel that the book is about real people. *Das Glasperlenspiel* has been an influential work which has reached a wide circle of readers in Germany.

The fiction of Ernst Wiechert (1887–1950) may be regarded as an act of mourning for the disappearance of the idyll from contemporary life. An elegiac mood runs through all this author's work, with its delineation of dark moods and emotional inwardness. His private sufferings under the Nazi régime and his sharing of the more general experience of the war period confirmed him in his longing for the quiet round of the solitary countryman and in his distrust of all organized forms of society. For his early work breathes the same nostalgia for the East Prussian countryside of his childhood which we find in his post-war work. An autobiographical account of his early years is entitled *Wälder und Menschen* ('Forests and People', 1936), and the simple life to which he refers in the novel *Das einfache Leben* (1939) is again a bucolic idyll. Like Hesse he has no patience with existing society, and in the short tale 'Der Hauptmann von Kapernaum' ('The Captain of Capernaum', 1930) he condemns militarism and the old order in Germany in the name of a non-institutional Christianity. After the war he wrote two large-scale works: the long epic of life in a remote East Prussian community, *Die Jerominkinder* ('The Jeromin Children', 1945-7), and the shorter and more effective *Missa sine Nomine* (1950). *Die Jerominkinder* traces the biographical development of the gifted son of a poor country family who goes to the Gymnasium in the nearest town, experiences the first world war as a medical orderly and, after finishing his studies, settles down in his native village as a general practitioner; the novel ends in the year 1939, with the community on the brink of new terrors. This book is less a portrait of an age than a document of the emotions, above all, of its author's omnipresent anxiety about the problem of evil in the world of a good Creator; the basis of the questioning is the Book of Job, and the quotation prefixed to the novel is the line 'With God is terrible majesty'. *Missa sine Nomine* has as its theme the rehabilitation of three brothers whose lives have been upset by events leading up to the end of the war in 1945. Ägidius soon finds stability in farming, Erasmus attempts unsuccessfully to devote himself to the welfare of displaced persons and refugees from the East, while Amadeus after the bitterness of four years in a concentration camp gradually acquires serenity and love. For Wiechert too confusion and suffering are to be relieved not primarily by reconstruction or organization, but at the less tangible level of a change of heart. Wiechert recalls Thomas Hardy in a number of his themes and moods—his love of nature and sensitivity to its atmosphere, his sense of pity, his predominantly autumnal and elegiacal view of the universe. Wiechert's characterization tends, however, to be stereotyped; his figures become too patently mouthpieces for his opinions. His emotional fervour too can degenerate into sentimentality, while his portrayal of erotic situations (as, for instance, the relationship between Amadeus and the seventeen-year-old Barbara in *Missa sine Nomine*) is not altogether happy. Wiechert's writing has indeed many weaknesses and stylistic lapses, but against these must be counted the emotional directness and the spontaneity of his idealism.

The *Novelle* by Hanna Stephan (born 1902), *Der Dritte* ('The Third Man'), recounts an episode during the flight of East Prussian country-people before the advance of the Russians in the winter of 1945. This tale is reminiscent of Wiechert's manner and motifs, just as Otto Heuschele's *Musik durchbricht die Nacht* ('Music Breaks Through the Night', 1956) recalls the lyrical restlessness of Hesse's work and expresses a comparable dissatisfaction with the industrial age. Bernt von Heiseler (born 1907) reflects more closely the atmosphere of Lutheran Protestantism in his work. *Apollonia* (1941), a love story in a peasant setting during the first world war, appears to be modelled on Gotthelf's tale of the French invasion of Switzerland in 1798, *Elsi, die seltsame Magd* ('Elsi, the Strange Maid'). *Versöhnung* ('Reconciliation', 1953) is a long *roman fleuve* showing the fortunes and misfortunes of a wide circle of friends during the Nazi period. Public events such as the assassination of Röhm in 1934, Neville Chamberlain's meetings with Hitler in 1938, the attempt on Hitler's life in 1944 and the defeat of Germany are neatly worked into a complex mesh of plot. A country estate in Bavaria forms the focal point in the lives of a family and their friends. Lutheran Christianity is in the forefront, though Heiseler has fewer misgivings than Wiechert in associating Christianity with the German upper-middle classes and a military tradition. The most convincing of the many plots and sub-plots which comprise the action is the account of a Lutheran pastor's struggles to maintain his integrity in face of political persecution.

Albrecht Goes (born 1908) has written morality plays, poetry and some prose, but he is not a prolific writer. Like Mörike, of whom he has written a short study, he is a native of Württemberg and a Protestant pastor. His two *Novellen* make an immediate impression by their direct sincerity and economy of presentation. *Unruhige Nacht* ('Unquiet Night', English translation 'Arrow to the Heart', 1949) narrates an episode from the campaign in Russia as seen by an army chaplain. *Das Brandopfer* ('The Burnt Offering', 1954) shows how a butcher's wife, while serving the weekly meat ration during the war, comes to realize fully the cruelty of the plight of Jews in Nazi Germany. The tale is a memorial, erected in a spirit of forgiveness, not of bitterness: 'To conjure up what has happened in the past; but for what purpose? Not in order to prolong hatred.' Goes' writing and care for form are precise, and his expression of an ideal of forgiveness and tolerance is framed in terms which have made these two tales compelling both to English and German readers.

The authors who have been mentioned in this chapter have not been experimental in language or in their approach to the novel form, and their realism prefers to dwell on country themes and to interpret contemporary problems with a hope of reconciliation and harmony. Even if by temperament sometimes inclined to despair, as Wiechert was, these writers attempt to realize a fundamental optimism of mood. They might be trying to think even today in terms of 'Der Bräutigam' ('The Bridegroom'), the poem of Goethe's old age, with its affirmatory closing line:

> Wie es auch sei das Leben, es ist gut.
> 'Life is good, whatever it is like.'

V

IRONY AND CONVICTION

In many ways Thomas Mann's earlier work was governed by an acceptance of Nietzsche's outlook and by the Neo-Romanticism of the eighteen-nineties. During the first world war Mann supported Imperialist Germany and interpreted the German spirit as conservative, romantic, musical, orderly, harmonious and spontaneous, in contradistinction to Western democracy which, he maintained, was based on equalitarian humanism and a rationalism which led to the glorification of the dissecting, sceptical intellect at the expense of the spirit. After much heart-searching in the light of Germany's defeat in 1918 Thomas Mann became a supporter of the Weimar Republic and social democracy; his interpretation of life in terms of a dichotomy between instinct and reason remained basically unchanged, but with increasing conviction he felt it was his duty to publicize his changed viewpoint and to preach the cause of rationalism and democracy as he understood them. His later writing became in consequence more didactic and discursive, and the greater part of his energies found expression in long novels which are intricate in structure and elaborate in style; the short stories and *Novellen* of the pre-1914 period are much more direct in approach and use of language.

Der Zauberberg ('The Magic Mountain', 1924) and the tetralogy *Joseph und seine Brüder* ('Joseph and his Brethren', 1933-43), the major works of the central period of their author's creative life, are both governed by a confidence in liberal humanism and in the reasonable possibility of progress. They are written in order to encourage the reader with a positive message, and it is thus not mere chance that they alone of their author's works conform with any closeness to the *Bildungsroman* in form. In contrast to the earlier artist-intellectual heroes, Hans Castorp is a simple, receptive

51

young man whose mind is moulded and ultimately improved by the educative factors in his environment, the Davos sanatorium, and especially by Naphta and Settembrini, the warring protagonists of evil and good, unconscious and conscious mind, dark and light, irrational and rational. In the 'snow scene' there comes for Hans Castorp a crucial moment of choice; he overcomes the temptation to drift towards death and asserts his intention to live, having arrived at this point at the conviction that death can only be defeated by kindness and love. *Joseph und seine Brüder* is a novel of an individual's development to a yet more consistent extent than *Der Zauberberg*. Joseph's sense of mission is repeatedly emphasized by the author, and though there are many subsidiary characters and many digressions, some entertaining and some tedious, Joseph remains central to the action, and as a personality is always more live and active than the shadowy Hans Castorp. He is a variant of the artist-hero; the imaginative odd-man-out among his half-brothers, with his sense of style and language and his enjoyment of learning and self-display, is taught by the sudden shock of his confinement to the well that artistry must be combined with cunning and the exploitation of charm if he is to become successful. The Bible story is rationalized, expanded, demythologized, indeed dehydrated, in the spirit of Freudian psychology interpreted in the light of Lessing and Goethe. Joseph is an artist and seer who becomes an administrator and economist, the most successful corn-dealer in ancient history. As the novel moves at leisurely pace to its cheerful ending, the author hints that his hero's sense of mission may have been motivated as much by vanity and ambition as by unselfish motives. In this his most grandiose work Thomas Mann plays with the then current themes of myth and psycho-analysis, seeking to render the dark forces harmless by laughing gently at them and to contain them, tamed by ridicule, within a world of enlightenment.

Doktor Faustus (1947) was by contrast directly topical when it appeared. It has been the most discussed political novel of recent years, a work which shows its author more alarmed on behalf of the future of democracy and liberal thought than ever before.

The mood of expansive tolerance has been replaced by a sharp hostility to Hitler's dictatorship which has been extended to aspects of German institutions as a whole. It is the biography of a fictitious musician, and thus a novel about an artist, but it unfolds a personality that ends in sterility and decay, not stability and maturity; the artistic temperament here is not adapted to the requirements of living in society, as was the case with Joseph, but becomes increasingly turned in upon itself. The daemonic forces swamp the 'flickering flame of the spirit'. Thomas Mann no longer puts a confident case for reason and worldly wisdom, but is an impassioned, comminatory prophet from the wilderness. The life-story of Adrian Leverkühn allows the author to recapitulate moods and tendencies in German society as he experienced them in the years before his own exile from Germany in 1933. Adrian was born in 1885, grows up in a middle-German small-town environment which represents a link with the experience of nineteenth-century German provincialism. His theological studies allow for satire at the expense of religious institutions, both Lutheran and Catholic, which are represented by teachers who are more interested in demonology than saintliness. Adrian's choice of music as his specialization is a fatal step towards complicity with the devil. In contrast to Hesse who sees in music the highest of the arts, Mann here regards music as a specifically German form of allurement towards evil. Adrian Leverkühn's preoccupation with musical composition is pursued persistently throughout the first world war, the period of inflation that followed, and the most hopeful years of the Weimar Republic; his indifference to social and political issues at a crucial period of modern German history is a further indication of an attitude that Mann deplores. The group of prosperous, cultured Bohemians who are his friends in and around Munich are shown as equally remote from the problems of their time, unless they have leanings to the extreme nationalism of the Kridwiss circle. With considerable liveliness Thomas Mann reconstructs the Germany he knew, so that *Doktor Faustus* may also be regarded as taking its place with the various other *romans fleuve* which have attempted a documentary reconstruction of a no longer existing form of German life.

The central chapter of the novel is a dialogue with the devil in which Adrian becomes aware that he has bought the ecstasies of artistic creativity and also the depths of depression with a pact that has been signed not in blood, but in venereal infection. Modelled on Ivan's confrontation with the devil in Dostoievsky's *The Brothers Karamazov*, this scene may be regarded as an illusion of Adrian's fevered mind rather than as the consequence of a corporeal manifestation. Mann's work is almost always kept within the bounds of everyday realism, but occasionally delusion and fantasy allow for a new dimension, in this pact scene as also, for instance, in the hypnotic suggestive powers of Cipolla in *Mario und der Zauberer* ('Mario and the Magician', 1929), a *Novelle* which in its criticism of Italian fascism anticipates *Doktor Faustus*. The price Adrian has to pay for inspiration derived from pride is complete isolation: 'You may not love . . . Your life is to be cold—therefore you may not love anyone.' By temperament Adrian is cool and undemonstrative, a man who retreats from emotional contact with other people, an uncommitted observer in all things except musical composition. But he tries twice to break the devil's bargain, when normal, simple human affection impels him to overcome the austerity of icy aestheticism. On both occasions it is a Swiss influence that kindles in him these warmer feelings; perhaps Mann wishes to emphasize the stability and democratic-bourgeois order of Switzerland, which for a number of years was the only example of a German-speaking community that was free from the hectic neuroses of Hitler's Germany. Adrian's love for the young Swiss woman, Marie Godeau, is shy and inhibited, and his own clumsiness loses her to his friend Rudi Schwerdtfeger; disaster supervenes with Rudi's assassination in a Munich tram, and Marie feels she can have no more contact with Adrian and his circle. This somewhat novelettish episode is less impressive than Adrian's affection for his nephew Nepomuk, the child of his sister who has married a Swiss optician. Adrian develops a spontaneous fondness for the five-year-old boy, being much affected by his innocence and Swiss-German talk. His feeling for the child is pure in a way that that of Aschenbach for Tadzio in *Der Tod in Venedig* certainly was not, and it is more appealing than that between Cornelius and his infant daughter Lorchen in the tale *Unordnung und frühes Leid* ('Disorder and Early Sorrow', 1926). But Nepomuk is unpredictably stricken with cerebro-spinal meningitis, and Adrian is confronted with the problem of suffering and evil in stark terms; as he watches the child die in the midst of intense pain, he is beset by pity and indignation, like Ivan Karamazov when he too is considering the sufferings of children, and ascribes his nephew's death to the machinations of the devil. The latter chapters of the novel are told with an increasing momentum, and the reader is hurtled along at a quick pace until the catastrophe where Adrian collapses at the piano, a victim of general paralysis of the insane, while he is ostensibly expounding his latest composition, 'Dr. Faustus' Lament', to his friends, though in fact he is recounting in a mixture of Swiss German and sixteenth-century German his own life-story seen as a pact with the devil. If *Der Zauberberg* and *Joseph* are novels of individual development, *Doktor Faustus* is an 'Anti-Bildungsroman', a parody and reversal of the didactic optimism of this traditional German novel form.

In earlier works Thomas Mann had frequently used myth, Wagnerian or Biblical, as background symbolism, and in *Doktor Faustus* he is of course taking up the semi-legendary figure of the sixteenth-century necromancer who, after the publication of Goethe's *Faust*, became a symbol in the nineteenth century for what was taken to be the specifically German contribution to modern life and thought. Mann deliberately by-passes Goethe's version in order to adhere more closely to the original conception of Faust in the chap-book of 1587. This account of the legend condemns Faust to hell for his pride and discontent. Thomas Mann also wishes to condemn the Faustian man and to emphasize how he differs in his interpretation from Goethe, who rescues his hero from the devil's clutches at death and who in the prologue in heaven causes the Lord to bless Faust's striving as being ultimately to a good end. Faust, the wanderer, the eagle, the amoral embodiment of sheer energy and curiosity, should be saved, as Goethe interpreted the legend; Mann was drawn to the simpler, black and white values of the anonymous author of the chap-book, and, in order to make the legend fit into his vision of its twentieth-century relevance, preferred to ignore the more sophisticated conception of Goethe.

The novel is a grim reckoning with Nietzsche, a recantation of the implications of his former guide's teaching. Adrian's life is in part based on incidents from Nietzsche's biography such as the visit to the brothel in Leipzig, the relationship with the prostitute Esmeralda, the subsequent feverish creative activity alternating with intense depression, and the final ten years of insanity. In the essay 'Nietzsches Philosophie im Lichte unserer Erfahrung' ('Nietzsche's Philosophy in the Light of Contemporary Events', 1947) Mann accuses Nietzsche of making two great mistakes. He assumed that reason was threatening to extinguish instinct, whereas, says Mann, the reverse is true, for the dark forces of unreason have never been more violent and dangerous than in the mid-twentieth century. He assumed also that morality was the enemy of instinctive life, but Mann asserts that the real opposites are ethics and aesthetics; not morality, but beauty is linked with death, and Nietzsche's attitude will lead to barbaric power-lust and the thirst for violence. While taking care to give credit to Nietzsche for his dislike of nationalism and anti-semitism, Mann does insist on the thesis that Nietzsche's philosophy, because of its emphasis on the aesthetic attitude, is close to barbarism and ashamed of the healthy values of truth, liberty and justice because they are bourgeois and not smart.

Adrian's musicianship is seen as a form of dabbling with the diabolic. His problem as a composer is parallel to the formal problems facing the European novelists at the end of the nineteenth century. The safe world of the realistic novelist gave way, after naturalism and Neo-Romanticism, to a feeling of insecurity that was not only metaphysical and social, but also a realization that the older style of straightforward narrative writing could no

longer be pursued without laying the author open to the charge
of derivative escapism. Similarly the resources of diatonic harmony
had largely been exhausted. Adrian's music teacher, Wendell
Kretschmar, expounds Beethoven's last piano sonata, which is
presented to us as an example of a daemonic German lack of
formal self-control breaking through the sonata form; it is
impressive, but disastrous, says Thomas Mann, and anticipates
romanticism in music, the chromaticism of Wagner and the
subsequent dissolution of traditional musical harmony. 'Why must
it seem to me as if almost all, in fact, all methods and devices of
the art are today only of use still for purposes of parody?' Adrian
asks. He becomes an atonal composer, and in order to have anything to say at all musically, he has to have the devil's help.

Adrian is thus to contain Faust, Nietzsche, the spirit of German
music, and indeed the German national character as a whole. In an
essay 'Deutschland und die Deutschen' ('Germany and the
Germans', 1945), Thomas Mann explains that he considers music
as symptomatic of all that he dislikes in his own countrymen:

Music is daemonic ground . . . It is at once most calculated order and
chaos-bearing anti-reason, full of spell-binding gestures of incantation,
magic of numbers, the art which is at once most remote from reality
and most impassioned, abstract and mystical. If Faust were to be the
representative of the German soul, he would have to be musical; for the
German's relation to the world is abstract and mystical, that is musical,
—the relationship of a professor with a touch of the daemonic, clumsy
and at the same time filled with arrogant consciousness of being
superior to the rest of the world in depth.

The issues of conflict are seen in much the same terms as in the
writing of Mann during the first world war, but now his faith is
fixed firmly in the cause of Western democracy:

The Germans are the people of the Romantic Counter-revolution
against the philosophical intellectualism and rationalism of the Age of
Enlightenment—of a revolt of music against literature, of mysticism
against clarity.

The narrator of the novel, Dr. Serenus Zeitblom, a teacher of

E   57

Classics, has been Adrian's devoted admirer and famulus from schooldays onwards. Like Settembrini in *Der Zauberberg*, Zeitblom can be discursively pedagogic, but at the same time he is his author's mouthpiece. After Adrian's death in 1940, the year of Hitler's most intoxicating triumphs, Zeitblom begins collecting biographical material about his friend and writes down the life-story between May 1943 and the last days of the Third Reich two years later. Adrian's pact with the devil and his decline into irremediable insanity are shown as parallel to Germany's increased isolation and exposure to bombing and invasion during the last two years of the war. There seems little hope for Germany at the end of *Doktor Faustus*, but the work does not exclude all possi-bility of regeneration. The final high cello note of 'Dr. Faustus' Lament' is intended to bear positive significance; and even if Adrian himself is lost, Zeitblom has survived, so that the voice of liberal humanism may yet be heard.

In spite of the elaborate style and structure and the lengthy disquisitions on music and other topics, Thomas Mann holds the reader's interest in his story; he remains a past master of his craft. The characterization is, however, less convincing; although Zeitblom is a credible and sympathetic, if irritating, narrator, Adrian Leverkühn lacks the stature demanded of the figure of a Faust, and few of the other characters are fully rounded.

The two works of fiction which follow *Doktor Faustus* are smaller in scale, much slighter in tone and texture, scurrilous and sarcastic, reminiscent of some minor but biting satire of Voltaire. *Der Erwählte* ('The Chosen One', English translation, 'The Holy Sinner', 1951) is a short novel which retells a medieval legend in the manner of a modern best-seller, with the embellishment of little linguistic jokes; the juxtaposition of American English and Middle High German may be intended to suggest the cosmo-politan nature of modern literature as being parodistically com-parable to the internationalism of medieval Christendom. Gregory, having been born in incest, grows up to marry his mother, then repents for seventeen years of self-imposed asceti-cism, until he is elevated to the Papacy, so that his wife and mother comes now to venerate him as 'father'. In this novel Mann, probably annoyed at German critics who had disliked his interpretation of the Faust legend, offers a sarcastic parody of the concept of salvation; with airy nonchalance Mann allows that grace may save the greatest sinner, and that the greater the sin, the more elevated will he become. By the time he came to write *Der Erwählte*, Western Germany was well on the way to economic recovery under Adenauer's Christian Democratic Party, which found little favour with Thomas Mann.

Die Betrogene ('The Deceived Woman', English translation, 'The Black Swan', 1953) is Thomas Mann's last afterthought on the German political situation. The setting of this *Novelle* is the period after the first world war. The figure of a middle-aged widow is the vehicle for the author's satire on the Conservative German middle-classes. Rosalie von Tümmler embodies a mixture of self-discipline, snobbery and easy emotionalism; she is a 'great friend of nature', just as Adrian Leverkühn was the musician *par excellence*. What she fancies as a reawakening to 'life' reveals itself as the advent of death in the shape of a haemorrhage precipitated by cancer of the womb. Rosalie is an ageing Germania, temporarily transmuted by flirtation with a vigorous, careless young American in the figure of Ken Keaton; but this 'miracle' of restoration is shortlived and only anticipates a complete and humiliating collapse. This clinical tale is a further indication of the sharpness of Mann's political feelings, but the mature humanity and serenity of *Joseph und seine Brüder* are sadly lacking here.

Felix Krull (1954), 'The confessions of a confidence-trickster', more than makes amends for the disappointing quality of the immediately preceding works. Here at last is the great German comic novel of our time, human and humorous, balanced and urbane, witty and uproarious, farcical and intelligent, a work in which scurrility is transformed into artistic achievement, not left as raw anger. With this first volume of a work that he did not live to complete, Mann reasserted his place as one of the greatest German novelists. This light, carefree comedy was begun much earlier in the author's career, at the time of *Der Tod in Venedig* and

Königliche Hoheit, and it is remarkable how Thomas Mann in his old age was able to recapture the deftness and agility of forty years earlier. It is a return to the earliest form of the modern novel, the picaresque novel of the sixteenth century. The rogue-hero is in the first place a device for unfolding a series of episodic adventures, and it is not his business to 'develop', but to come through his experiences unscathed and unchanged. Whereas the hero of the *Bildungsroman* is earnest, idealistic and often unenterprising, like Wilhelm Meister or Hans Castorp, the picaresque hero lives by his wits and is untroubled by moral scruples or by any desire to improve himself culturally. Felix' family background is not the sober, solid Protestant North German milieu of Hans Castorp or Tonio Kröger, but that of the Catholic Rhineland where his father manufactures bad champagne. He becomes a deceiver because of his artistic temperament which, like Joseph, he exploits in order to make society give him what he wants. One of Mann's favourite themes has been the closeness of artistic inspiration to disease. Felix 'improves on nature' when he learns how to sham illness to serve his own ends, as in the richly comic scene of his appearance before the military medical board. He is the happy wanderer who takes the earliest available opportunity to shake the dust of the fatherland off his feet and to find a more congenial and stimulating jumping-off ground for his adventures in Paris. As a waiter in a hotel he has opportunities to marry a young woman from Birmingham and to accompany an older man to aristocratic solitude in the Highlands, but he resists these temptations to return to a quasi-Germanic environment and is rewarded by the more exciting offer of proceeding to Portugal under an assumed noble identity. It is not until the journey to the south begins that the full picaresque machinery is set in motion, and Felix enters the 'great world'.

He is attractive to women, and the two principal erotic escapades in the book are with older women. But Felix' adventures are kept consistently on the level of Rococo comedy, and love plays no serious part in his life. Situations which in previous works had been treated with seriousness and undertones of the daemonic are here presented without sinister implications as sheer entertainment. The happiest moment in his life, Felix decides, as he looks back during his leisure in prison, was the afternoon when at the age of eight he was provided with a toy violin and extravagant clothes and allowed to mimic in public the performance of a Hungarian dance by a member of a café orchestra. 'Music enchants me, indeed, although I have never taken the opportunity of learning to perform, this dreamy art possesses in me a fanatical adorer . . .' Music does not bring danger to Felix, but the most complete success the small boy could imagine: compliments, flattery, embraces, an expensive present, a free treat of cream-cakes and drinking chocolate, and the respectful attention of other children. Felix is a less scrupulous Joseph to whom Paris in the nineties opens up a new life comparable to the Egypt of the Pharaohs. His adventures make a vigorous, inventive and urbane novel which will take a high place in that body of work which has won Thomas Mann his literary position of European and world significance. Tiresome and irritating his writing may be on occasions, so that we are uncertain whether he is a conjuror or a magician, but he has commanded attention for sixty years, both as teacher and entertainer, and his eminence as a leading novelist of the twentieth century is firmly established.

VI

'THE GOLDEN FUTURE TIME'

THE Utopian novel has had a considerable vogue in Germany in
the recent past, and Hermann Hesse's *Das Glasperlenspiel*, in con-
junction with Ernst Jünger's *Auf den Marmorklippen*, may be
taken as having initiated the revival of this genre of fiction in
Germany. The wish to write about topical issues at the end of the
war was not limited to Thomas Mann, though *Doktor Faustus*
remains the most outstanding of this type of novel, nor to the
semi-documentary fiction which was mentioned earlier in this
essay; a number of writers who had similar urges expressed them
in the form of novels about the future. Few of these works may
be called Utopias in any exact sense, for they are seldom optimistic enough to depict the ideal state as something to be achieved
in time by good will and common sense; we are far removed
from the Pre-Raphaelite idealism of William Morris' *News from
Nowhere*, or even from the less comfortable vision of Samuel
Butler's *Erewhon*. If H. G. Wells was on occasions able to write
about the future in a spirit of scientific optimism, he too had many
misgivings, and tales like *The Time Machine* and *When the Sleeper
Awakes* show a sensitivity and anxiety quite as observant as the
fantasies by later writers who have had the events of world
history since 1939 to draw upon for their material. Aldous
Huxley's fears for the future were very different in *Brave New
World* (1932), where scientific progress was to produce a world
of material comfort without mind or passion, from the wholly
unrelieved pessimism about a post-atomic future shown in the
hastily written later fantasy *Ape and Essence* (1949). Of all contemporary visions of the future, George Orwell's *1984* has had
the most immediate impact on Germany, as elsewhere. The
'golden future time' which the beasts in *Animal Farm* chant in

chorus is a theme which preoccupied Orwell for many years; his essays on H. G. Wells and Arthur Koestler testify to this, as well as the passages on socialism and the future in *The Road to Wigan Pier* (1937). Any study of fantasy-world fiction in our time would have to give pride of place to Orwell's particular form of irony.

Oskar Maria Graf (born 1894) wrote his 'novel of a future', *Die Eroberung einer Welt* ('The Conquest of a World', 1948), in America before the end of the second world war. It is an example of a type of straightforwardly didactic writing that seems old-fashioned by comparison with H. G. Wells' better work. The story envisages a chaotic situation at the conclusion of world war three which is eventually resolved by the establishment of a humane world government.

Franz Werfel (1890–1945) turned to novel writing in middle life, after making his name in the vanguard of the Expressionist movement primarily with verse and drama. Religious themes had already played some part in his work before the popular success of *Das Lied von Bernadette* ('The Song of Bernadette', 1941) made this story of healing at Lourdes a best-seller. His last novel was a vision of life 100,000 years ahead, *Stern der Un-geborenen* ('Star of the Unborn', 1945), which is concerned with somewhat the same problems as Hesse's *Das Glasperlenspiel*. They are, however, stated in a different manner. Werfel is more circumstantial in the way he builds up his picture of the future, though his writing is loose and shapeless. He clearly enjoyed speculating on the details of possible intellectual and technical developments, and his descriptions of inter-planetary travel remind us of science fiction. In its Californian background, its spiritual-istic framework and its general approach to intellectual problems, *Stern der Ungeborenen* has something of Aldous Huxley's *Time Must Have a Stop* and the earlier *Brave New World*. Werfel portrays a world-state which has been in existence in its present refined and comfortable way for many centuries. Life is longer, but the world population is smaller, and each individual is more precious and more delicate. There are material comforts for all, and harmless games. This civilization is, however, threatened with collapse through the extension of the 'jungle' reservations, tracts of land inhabited by primitives of a twentieth-century type. The 'astromental' world is finally overrun by the jungle dwellers, and for the most part its inhabitants choose suicide in face of this situation. Werfel's portrayal of an over-refined civilization that collapses before a new assertion of instinctive vitality is more credible and colourful than Hesse's *Das Glasperlenspiel*; but for all the cleverness of much of the fantasy, *Stern der Ungeborenen* remains wordy and long drawn-out. The posthumously collected three volumes of shorter tales, *Erzählungen aus zwei Welten* ('Stories from Two Worlds', 1948–54), contain much ephemeral material; the better stories are those which date back to the time when Werfel was prominent as an Expressionist.

Die Stadt hinter dem Strom ('The City beyond the River', 1947), by Hermann Kasack (born 1896), is a vision not of the future, but of life after death. There is, however, as in *Stern der Ungeborenen*, a carefully constructed fantasy world, run according to its own laws, which bewilders the stranger who finds himself plunged into it. Robert Lindhoff feels himself alien to the structure of life in this perplexing town, where most activities are carried on underground, while the streets above are mostly deserted and the houses in ruins. He cannot understand the reasons that compel subservience to a mysterious higher authority. The theme of the odd man out in an alien, puzzling world is one of the many pointers that show Kasack's indebtedness to Kafka. It is not until half way through the book, after the love scene with Anna, that Lindhoff discovers that he is the only living person in a city of the dead, and that the others have only a short time to wait before their spirits are dissolved in the All. Like Hesse, Kasack feels drawn to Eastern mysticism, and expounds his vision of the relationship of life and death in pantheistic terms. Western civilization in the twentieth century is heading for disaster, and the world can only be saved by a re-establishment of the spiritual and intellectual supremacy of the East, which shall counter 'the deadly poison of reason' and the misuse of technological inventions. The earlier half of the book, where Lindhoff is introduced to conditions in the city, keeps up the suspense well, and the description is rounded and plastic. The later sections, where political and social satire plays a large part and where the philosophical system of the book is expounded in more detail, are abstract and lacking in tension. Although Kasack's statement of dilemma evidently lacks the intensity of vision of Kafka's work, *Die Stadt hinter dem Strom* remains a competent, talented work. His more recent novel *Das große Netz* ('The Big Net', 1952), a lengthy satire about the demoralizing effects of a materialistic hedonism in the Hollywood style, is much less interesting.

Walter Jens (born 1923) is less concerned in his novel about the future with the wider philosophical issues that Hesse, Kasack or Werfel discuss in their fantasies. *Nein. Die Welt der Angeklagten* ('No. The World of the Accused', 1950) is a straightforward plea for political freedom. The world-state has divided mankind into three classes—judges, witnesses and plaintiffs; it is run by a system of secret police-spying that reduces humanity to a collection of scared automata incapable of independent thought or unselfish impulse. This novel has resemblance to Orwell's *1984* or Kafka. Jens' subsequent story *Der Blinde* ('The Blind Man', 1951) describes the reactions of a man in middle life who finds himself confronted by sudden blindness. A novel *Vergessene Gesichter* ('Forgotten Faces', 1952) is concerned with the inmates of a home for retired actors. *Der Mann, der nicht alt werden wollte* ('The Man who did not want to grow Old', 1955) is another novel. It is a satire on German academic methods which are used by a retired university professor to unravel the motives underlying the suicide of one of his former students.

Arno Schmidt (born 1910) is a satirist, corrosive in his pessimism and remarkably effective in his visual impressions. He writes in a laconic, concentrated style, usually taking the diary form as the basis for his narrative. Events are seen through the eyes of a disgruntled, down-at-heel intellectual, full of bile but void of self-pity. The volume *Leviathan* (1949) contains an acid sketch of a train journey out of Berlin in February 1945. A curiously assorted group of individuals commandeer a locomotive and a carriage, and set off on an illicit journey eastwards, only to meet death. *Brand's Haide* ('Brand Heath', 1951) is the account of a dis-illusioned ex-soldier who settles down to be a writer in conditions of destitution in 1946. He finds happiness in love, until his mistress deserts him to marry an American. For him there is only slight consolation in her promise to send him food parcels, and he is left in a mood that is, typically enough, 'empty and dull grey'. Schmidt continues his poker-faced, staccato jabbing at the con-dition of humanity in *Aus dem Leben eines Fauns* ('From the Life of a Faun', 1953). Here is a satire on German urban provincial life in 1939; its destruction by bombing in 1944 was no great loss, is its implication. 'Each writer should grasp the nettle reality, and show us everything', we are told. Most drastic of Schmidt's sketches is his vision of the future 'Schwarze Spiegel' ('Black Mirrors', in the volume *Brand's Haide*). Here the author realizes the dream that his protagonist was toying with in *Leviathan*, the destruction of the human race. We are presented a central Europe in 1962 after a war that leaves alive only one man and one woman. It may be a garden of Eden made for two, but there are limita-tions. This tale incidentally parodies fantasy-world fiction in general, and in particular the works of Kasack and Jens.

A large-scale political fantasy is being written by Stefan Andres (born 1906), a prolific writer who has been publishing since 1928. The first novel, *Bruder Luzifer* ('Brother Lucifer', 1932), is about a young artist who enters a Capucine order as a novice, but leaves after a year. One of the author's recurring themes is brought out here; the conflict between the moral order, as understood by Roman Catholicism, and the strong appeal of the senses. There is a certain conventionality of theme and treatment in the stories of love and art set in a Mediterranean background which Andres wrote in the nineteen-thirties. In the novella *Wir sind Utopia* ('We are Utopia', 1942), which was forbidden publication in wartime Germany but was clandestinely circulated at the time, Andres sub-ordinated erotic preoccupations to a consideration of social and political issues. This tale about the Spanish civil war is probably the author's best-known work. The central character is a man who gives up life as a monk in order to work for his vision of an ideal world. An older priest echoes Andres' view when he tells him: 'Nobody has yet been able to reform the world and make a Utopia of it, nobody, not even God Himself! . . . He loves this world because it is imperfect.' Since 1945 Andres has continued to emphasize the element of social and political criticism in his fiction. *Die Hochzeit der Feinde* ('The Marriage of the Enemies', 1947) treats the problem of Franco-German relationships, and *Ritter der Gerechtigkeit* ('Knights of Justice', 1948) is set in Italy at the time of the fall of Mussolini. *Die Sintflut* ('The Flood') is planned as a trilogy of which two parts, *Das Tier aus der Tiefe* ('The Beast from the Depths', 1949) and *Die Arche* ('The Ark', 1951), have so far been published. In the introductory chapter Andres explains his intention as the description of the Flood of our time, that is, the Nazi dictatorship. His method is one of realism, but in a Utopian setting, for he wishes to avoid the approach of complete fantasy on the one hand and topical political reporting on the other: 'For the historical novel tries to awaken the dead, while journalism contents itself with the arrangement of what is already decaying.' Although it is a tale of corruption and greed for power, *Das Tier aus der Tiefe* is full of humour—and not the intellectual wit of G. B. Shaw, but the full-blooded humour of Dickens, as G. K. Chesterton distinguished them. The plot is sustained in its many ramifications, and if the sense of its inevitability is sometimes lacking, the author jumps clean over the gap with his exuberant fantasy. The first volume shows the rise of the party from obscure origins under the leadership of Andres' archetypal dictator, the ex-priest Dr. Alois Moosthaler. The second volume covers the period from the dictator's seizure of power in Germany to the time shortly before the outbreak of a major war. Moosthaler and his satellites are no longer in the foreground, which is unfortunate as the pace of the novel becomes less assured in consequence. The chief theme is now the suffering of a group of independent spirits who refuse to conform to the régime of the newly established dictator. *Die Reise nach Portiuncula* ('The Journey to Portiuncula', 1954) is a novel on a much less ambitious scale than the *Sintflut* volumes, but is none the less colourful and vivid. A prosperous middle-aged German brewer takes a holiday in Italy and returns to the place where thirty years before he betrayed a simple Italian girl and, with her, his youthful ideals of Franciscan poverty. Sulpiz Kasbach is a clever and rounded portrait of a German business man of the nineteen-fifties. By the quality and variety of the work he has already produced, Stefan Andres has established himself as a lively and immediately engaging novelist.

Ernst Jünger (born 1895) has for a long time, since the appearance of his books on his experiences during the first world war, been concerned with problems of man and society. Aloof and solitary, he has gone his own way through the vicissitudes of the last forty years in Germany with fair consistency of outlook and reactions, hesitating to associate himself with any large-scale organized movements, political or religious, and developing from Nietzschean thought his own conception of a leadership that shall combine worldly power with an aristocratic aestheticism. Coldly and analytically he has dwelt on situations involving pain, violence and death. His diagnoses on the lot of modern man may be motivated by an ultimate desire to help and to heal, but he is reluctant to make any such motives at all obvious, and one need have no regrets that he has never been let loose to operate on the patient. His four recent fictional works, all translations of contemporary problems into a fantasy world setting, are interesting primarily for the stylistic details of their prose and for the dry, clever presentation of ideas, rather than for their characterization or narrative; the backgrounds too are implausible, even if described with meticulous care. *Auf den Marmorklippen* ('On the Marble Cliffs', 1939) and *Heliopolis* (1949) have in common the theme of a fight between a minority of aristocratic intellectuals and the cunningly organized forces of a mass dictatorship. The two brothers in *Auf den Marmorklippen* are forced out of their studious seclusion by the insidious encroachments of the Chief Forester and align themselves with Braquemart who, icy and full of hate, sees mankind in two classes, noble supermen and slaves, and who wishes to overthrown the Chief Forester because of his plebeian threat to the aristocracy's independence as much as on account of the cruelties of his concentration camp. The brothers escape to Alta Plana, where as refugees they wish to work against the Chief Forester, while in *Heliopolis*, the longest of Jünger's fictional works, Lucius de Geer and his wife have to leave the scene of conflict in order to assume new responsibilities on behalf of the Prokonsul. Set in the remote future, *Heliopolis* contains detailed accounts of the material amenities of life and the widening of knowledge since the twentieth century; like Hesse in *Das Glasperlenspiel*, Jünger seems here to be seeking links with the German classical-romantic novel, in particular with Goethe's *Wilhelm Meister*. Life has taken on a new shape with the discovery of new worlds and the possibility of living there, but in spite of space travel, humanity is still frozen in the old gestures of conflict. After a period of settled comfort for all there comes a renaissance of nihilism, a large-scale war between believers in technology and those with faith in the spirit. Lucius de Geer, the central character, sees conflict as inevitable to human life:

In long times of peace, annoyance, unrest and tedium vitae spread like a fever. There had to be, perhaps ever since the time of Cain and Abel, two great races, each with a wholly different conception of happiness. And both continued to exist in mankind, taking the leadership by turn. Often both of them dwelt in the same breast.

Heliopolis shows mind and violence in a state of tension, but not open warfare, and there is no question of the Mauretanians, with their Platonic values, military hierarchy and intellectual vigour, being destroyed by the unscrupulous tyranny of the Landvogt. Thus it is a more optimistic book than *Auf den Marmorklippen*, where the brutality of the Chief Forester is so much in the ascendant. *Heliopolis* contains a wealth of material that provides a stimulating discussion of wide issues, but, apart from the inset story 'Ortners Erzählung', the narrative gets clogged up, and the private life of Lucius de Geer, his relations with the two women Melitta and Budur Peri, remains remote. Jünger's highly polished style is here a barrier to the achievement of a convincing novel, just as George Meredith's self-conscious prose was one factor that prevented his ingenious and energetic writing from receiving general appreciation.

Besuch auf Godenholm ('Visit to Godenholm', 1952) and *Gläserne Bienen* ('Glass Bees', 1957) do not describe a world in conflict, but a post-war situation as seen by ex-soldiers who are resentful of the loss of prestige and meaning in their lives caused by defeat and the redundancy of their military training. The two protagonists of *Besuch auf Godenholm* are to be rescued from the nihilism which has assailed them in post-war Germany by a visit to a Norwegian island where blind submission to a sage-magician, whose daemonic personality is rooted obscurely in Germanic mythology, provides them with a hidden power which is to restore meaning to their lives. *Gläserne Bienen* uses the same skeleton action, this time in order to attack the all-pervasive seeping of commercialized monopoly-controlled technology into modern life; the implications of this tale were foreshadowed in Jünger's sociological study *Der Arbeiter* ('The Worker', 1932). Richard, an ex-cavalry officer, has an obsessive nostalgia for horses and a distrust of working men from Manchester and Sheffield; on his uppers after the defeat of Germany in 1918, he asks an old crony to find him a job with good money in order to prevent him from succumbing to what he regards as degrading routine. After being given a breakfast which includes toast, ham and eggs, tea and port wine, Richard is sent off with a fifty-pound note to the organization of Zapparoni, a tycoon and grey eminence whose children's films and mechanical toys assure him mass popularity and create an aura of harmlessness about scientific inventions which may at the same time be used as weapons of mass destruction. Zapparoni has built his streamlined industrial premises around an old Cistercian monastery, where in the centre of his organization he may enclose himself in a carefully constructed atmosphere of traditional culture. The great man arouses in Richard the longing to abase himself and to obey him implicitly, but the protagonist has misgivings and the suspicion that the ease and pleasures that he will now be able to buy will be acquired at the price of slavery to an unscrupulous nihilism. Zapparoni's inventions are 'the cowardly triumph of calculating brains over courage and life'. Richard is left alone in the midday warmth of a garden where he is started out of a nap to discover that the bees around him are robots and that an ornamental pool is afloat with human ears which, however, on closer inspection turn out to be synthetic. Jünger's botanizing, which recurs frequently in his writings, here takes on a surrealist tone. Although he realizes that this ordeal is a test of his suitability for the work, Richard expresses his revulsion and prepares to defy Zapparoni. The latter, however, is not easy to offend, and offers him not the important job he had in mind for him, but a less impressive one. Richard accepts—he has a wife to support—and thus his gesture of defiance is transformed into a reluctant, but inevitable acceptance of the smug mediocrity of mechanized conformity. *Gläserne Bienen* is a curious book, undeniably topical in its social criticism. Human perfection and technological virtuosity are irreconcilable, the hero reflects. 'An uncanny but also fascinating brilliance lights up perfect mechanisms. They arouse fear, but also a titanic pride which can be brought low not by insight, but only by catastrophe.' The satire is not altogether negative, and there is a longing for moral standards, a rule to live by: 'We are all burningly concerned with the thought that after all there may still be a hope'. This satire of short novel length is the most compelling of the author's imaginative works since *Auf den Marmorklippen*. Jünger may well be claimed as the outstanding practitioner of Utopian fiction in modern German literature.

VII

THE OBSERVERS

SWITZERLAND's policy of democratic neutrality has been maintained through the turmoils of the two twentieth-century European wars. With German, French and Italian as officially recognized languages, its national individuality has never depended on any narrow racial or linguistic bonds. Although an immediate neighbour of Germany and Austria, Switzerland has been an observer of the violent changes and upheavals experienced by these countries, but has itself remained apart from them and retained a consistency in its social life which other countries often envy.

Unless we reckon Hermann Hesse as a Swiss author, the most distinguished prose-stylist of the earlier years of the present century was Robert Walser (1878–1956). His prose reveals a sensitive, retiring, whimsical man, gently ironical at the expense of pretentiousness and cut-and-dried living, devoted to his ideal of art, dreamer, wanderer, minute observer of the Swiss countryside, of children and ordinary life, and always ready to let everyday reality dissolve into fantasy. Walser's work is impressionistic in method, and it suffers chiefly from paucity of action and characterization; a tendency to tenuousness and repetitiveness is to be noticed. Light, lyrical, delicate and witty, with an easy, gentle irony, Walser's style has affinities with that of the early stories of Hesse or of Kafka's sketches and fables. Kafka was almost certainly influenced by Walser's manner, both in the form of his shorter sketches as also in his technique of taking the familiar detail of everyday life as the jumping-off ground for fantasy.

But Walser's whimsical rebelliousness against the sober routine of middle-class life is not echoed by all Swiss authors. Some of them accept the society in which they have grown up, a society which has been exposed to no sudden shocks of intrusion or violence for over a hundred years, as a responsibility and an ethical obligation. This is the main message that emerges from novels by writers such as Inglin, Kübler or Guggenheim. Meinrad Inglin (born 1893) has continued in the tradition of solid, three-dimensional realism combined with a sense of service to the community which is characteristic of the two major Swiss novelists of the nineteenth century, Gotthelf and Keller. *Der Schweizerspiegel* ('The Swiss Mirror', 1938) is a family saga and a picture of Swiss society from 1912 to 1918. *Werner Amberg* (1949) is a *Bildungsroman* with a probably autobiographical basis, showing clear affinities with Keller's *Der grüne Heinrich*. The collection of tales *Die Lawine* ('The Avalanche', 1947) again illustrates the careful, weighty style of his writing. The puniness of man, in the twentieth century as well as in any other age, before the elemental furies of the mountains is the theme of the story which gives the title to this collection and also of the stark 'Drei Männer im Schneesturm' ('Three Men in the Snowstorm').

Alfred Kübler (born 1890) published in 1939 a collection of short stories *Das Herz—Die Ecke—Der Esel* ('The Heart, the Corner, the Donkey') which show with their deprecatory irony his affinity with the humorous vein of Keller's writing. His major work is the long novel of individual development *Öppi* ('Someone'), which has appeared in three volumes between 1943 and 1951. With its setting in Switzerland in the early years of the present century, this novel gives a careful reconstruction of the atmosphere of a now irrevocably bygone age that reminds us of Max René Hesse's *Dietrich Kattenburg* or Carossa's autobiography. The loss of his mother when he is twelve is the psychological bruise which is to affect the development of the boy Öppi from this time onwards. He is one of a large family, and his father, innkeeper and timber-merchant in a small village, goes about his own busy and upright life content to leave the youngest child alone, provided he does not get in his father's way. But the boy feels starved of affection, without fully realizing that this is the case, and without being able to find a satisfactory alternative to the maternal warmth he misses. Through this he is alienated from his family, and when he goes to the *Gymnasium* to embark on a classical education he is further separated from the non-intellectual community life of the village. He has risen above his family and village by taking up an academic education, but always remains defiantly mistrustful of much that middle-class urban education stands for. Caught in this social dilemma, he responds by identifying himself with village activities and seeking, for instance, in the local gymnastic club a sense of community which he misses in the town school. Aroused to enthusiasm for science by his headmaster, Öppi becomes, in the second volume of the saga, a student of geology at a university town which is presumably Zürich. The crisis in Öppi's student life occurs after he has taken a term off to visit Italy; dissatisfied with the field of study he has been pursuing so far, he abandons geology to take up art. The situation is that of Keller's 'Green Heinrich' in Munich; but in Kübler's novel it is not art but science which proves to be the false vocation. The war of 1914–18 presents another dilemma; although the world outside is caught up in a chaos of tension and catastrophe, he as a Swiss can choose to remain apart. His own slow development is allowed to take its course. He tries drawing and sculpture, only to turn away in order to seek a career as an actor. The third volume centres upon his love affair with Eva, a woman from North Germany, who awakens Öppi to emotional maturity. At this point the novel ends. Öppi is still hesitating, having achieved little or nothing in the way of outward success; but he has become a full man, in the sense which the traditional *Bildungsroman* likes to emphasize. The dilettantism has not been for nothing, we are given to understand; the apprenticeship is over, though the mastery remains a matter for the future. Kübler's unfolding of the story of his hero is slow and sure, indeed one could wish for a more sprightly and ironical approach towards the material. With its large panorama of life in village and town, the work gives an impressively comprehensive picture of Swiss society a generation or so ago.

Kurt Guggenheim (born 1896) has also tackled the psychological problems brought about by life in a small, stable community which has little room for outsiders. His recent novel *Der Friede des Herzens* ('Peace of Heart', 1956) takes as its hero a middle-aged man who has always been painstaking and quietly conscientious in the routine of the insurance office which fills up his working hours, and devoted in his leisure time to his wife, daughter and respectable flat. He attempts to break through the frustrations of the planned prosperity which encloses him on all sides, but fails. His rebellion brings disaster to the woman who becomes his mistress, while he himself, even if only obliquely hurt, has inner conflicts to wrestle with before he finally becomes reconciled to the outward sameness of his life.

The three tales of Hans Walter, *Im Verborgenen* ('On the Quiet', 1950), depict the surface banality of small-town or village settings, an asphyxiatingly unruffled social background which exacerbates suspicions and latent tensions until tragedy is imminent. Carl J. Burckhardt's volume of *Drei Erzählungen* (1952) contains two stories which link Swiss background and reactions to the indirect impact of the last war. Burckhardt has an urbanity of style and a quiet, human sympathy which give his stories an attractive smoothness of finish; they are at once regional and universal in scope. His personal friendship with Hugo von Hofmannsthal is recorded in their correspondence during the years from 1919 to the older man's death (*Hugo von Hofmannsthal, Carl J. Burckhardt: Briefwechsel*, 1956). Burckhardt speaks here for Swiss civilization in terms which are comparable to the way in which Hofmannsthal became the definitive and representative figure of Austrian culture during these years. These letters are a commentary on their time and their authors; Hofmannsthal expresses his fears that with the disappearance of the old order bleak chaos alone will supervene, while Burckhardt refuses to despair of the combined tradition of Christianity and classical humanism. In a letter of August 1928 Hofmannsthal writes:

I have missed your company too much this whole year—the climate of your mind which is so related and so beneficial to mine. Something very deep is common to us, this urge to grasp all and to conserve—but around this deepest point there is still an infinite sense of companionship.

The Austrian goes on to recount in this context the deep impression that the reading of Gotthelf's tale 'Der Sonntag des Großvaters' ('The Grandfather's Sunday') has made upon him.

The two contemporary German-Swiss authors who have become best known outside their own country are Friedrich Dürrenmatt (born 1921) and Max Frisch (born 1911). Both are critical of any complacent taking-for-granted of contemporary Switzerland. Dürrenmatt is the author of a number of lively dramas influenced by French existentialism which are full of ideas and variety of character and situation; *Ein Engel kommt nach Babylon* ('An Angel Comes to Babylon', 1954) is a comedy with something of the fantastic buoyancy of G. B. Shaw's earlier work. *Die Ehe des Herrn Mississippi* ('The Marriage of Mr. Mississippi', 1952) and *Der Besuch der alten Dame* ('The Old Lady's Visit', 1956) have also already become well established as stage-plays. In prose fiction Dürrenmatt has confined himself to neatly contrived light entertainment as in his two detective stories *Der Richter und sein Henker* ('The Judge and his Hangman', 1952) and *Der Verdacht* ('Suspicion', 1953).

Max Frisch is also a playwright; his satire on dictators, *Die chinesische Mauer* ('The Chinese Wall', 1946), was revived in Berlin in 1955, and a comedy, *Don Juan*, was produced in English translation in Bristol in 1956. His novel *Stiller* (1954) regards the Swiss tradition coldly and satirically. It is concerned in the first place with the relationships of a self-conscious individual to those with whom his life is bound; the broader theme, a critique of mid-twentieth-century civilization from a Swiss point of view, is built up by inference and satirical incident. The conventions of a society that knows that it is reasoned, sensible, economically sound and traditionally democratic make Stiller rebel against the prearranged pattern of career and family. But he is not Promethean in his defiance. As a sculptor he was undistinguished, and he has no inclination to exploit his talents for commercial success. His preliminary breaking-loose as a volunteer in the Spanish civil war has led to a further lack of faith in himself as well as in the cause which he wished to defend. His marriage to a promising ballerina leads to misunderstandings and jealousy of her success; when she becomes ill with tuberculosis, he is indifferent and unfaithful. He disappears to America, where he lives for six years, nomadic and at times near to suicide, but at least, the implication is, in places where life can be raw and unpredictable. While travelling through Switzerland on a forged American passport, Stiller is arrested by police authorities who conscientiously set about proving that he is the person whose identity he rejects. His dentist can demonstrate his identity from the state of his teeth, the army authorities deplore the shocking state of his military equipment after six years' neglect, while there is the suspicion that he has had connexions with Russian espionage. The court of inquiry decides that he is Stiller, whether he like it or not, and makes him pay a carefully and fairly calculated fine to cover the expense and trouble that he has caused the authorities. There is an extended account of Stiller's alcoholic inertia and depression after the death of his wife, with whom he effects a reconciliation after the court of inquiry is concluded; this is hardly consistent with the comedy of the opening sections of the novel. At one point Stiller asks himself if his personality and his experiences are real, or to what extent they are second-hand. Does he know Spain through Hemingway, Mexico through Graham Greene, Paris through Ernst Jünger, and so on? And what else has he got from Kafka and Thomas Mann? Max Frisch's novel is written throughout with a self-conscious narrative technique, and motifs and mannerisms from numerous contemporary sources have been exploited. It has a cosmopolitan polish and an easy urbanity, while remaining unmistakably Swiss.

In such authors as these Swiss writing goes on its own way, with a firm grip on the realities of everyday life and an avoidance of extravagant gesture, though at its best always aware, both with irony and sympathy, of the closeness one to another of all European problems in our time.

VIII

SURREALISM

IMAGINATIVE writing which aims to gain new vistas of life by breaking down the walls of objective realism in order to admit a new dimension of vision asserted itself at the turn of the century with the Neo-Romantic movement; and Kafka's writing may be regarded as reflecting an Expressionist interpretation of this experiment. André Breton's *Manifeste du Surréalisme* (1924) consciously summoned a new literary school into being, though the words 'surréalisme' had been coined earlier by Guillaume Apollinaire. Axiomatic to the surrealist was a mistrust of logical reasoning and an almost mystical belief in a higher reality which is revealed in dreams, abnormal mental states and generally through the unconscious mind. The influence of Freud on the French surrealists is evident, and especially when we bear in mind that André Breton was himself a specialist in nervous diseases. These were the years too when James Joyce was living in Paris and had recently published his *Ulysses*. The surrealist's aim was to break down the prison-bars of the world of reason and common sense, which atrophied or distorted the lives of so many adults; only children could still see the world around as enchanted and miraculous. The social and political implications of surrealism were an outspoken opposition to all that was traditional. In personal life bohemianism and sexual emancipation were advocated, while anarchism or political revolution were to sweep away the outworn framework of society. Very many contemporary German writers have been affected by this heightening of realism by the intermingling of conscious and unconscious experience, even if they do not always speak of surrealism or 'magic realism'. In part too it is a romantic movement, and the German exponents of surrealism invoke Novalis and Brentano, Jean Paul and E. T. A.

Hoffmann, though the shadow of Kafka falls more urgently across their writings.

In a letter from Berlin of 28 March 1945, Friedo Lampe (1899–1945) wrote:

What times these are! I try more and more to regard this age and its terrible happenings as a process of purification. We should say goodbye to everything, be bound no longer to what is earthly, and should look at life as if we had already died. We should learn to conquer fear of life as of death. The hope of a sensible and happier life is surely very slight. The whole of Germany is after all a heap of rubble. Continuity with the past has been destroyed. None of this can be made good again. No, we may not think further along these lines. We must learn to think on other lines, but that is very painful and difficult, especially for people like myself who live through sense impressions. Right at the end may be seen beckoning a freedom and happiness, a feeling of being separated from all that is material, and an insight into the infirmity and transience of earthly things which earlier generations have experienced only in rare comparable moments.

Shock, bewilderment, a sense of loss and a yearning to be made clean are expressed here. The author of these lines, which were penned no doubt in distracted haste and anguish, reflects in his few, but delightfully written stories a spirit of sensitive fantasy and humour that recalls the manner of Robert Walser. Essentially a minor writer, unimportant enough to be left alone by the Third Reich, his work has only become known at all widely in the volume of his *Gesamtwerk*, ('Collected Works', 1955) since his death. For he was shot by Russian troops on 2 May 1945, through a misunderstanding in the first days after the Russian occupation of Berlin. His sparkling, iridescent prose reflects atmosphere, colour and the sensation of things, as in the short story 'Am Leuchtturm' ('At the Lighthouse'), where butterfly impressions of a summer day at a North Sea seaside resort are neatly and cleanly pinned down.

Like Friedo Lampe, Ernst Kreuder (born 1903) is concerned with the vindication of fantasy as such. *Die Gesellschaft vom Dach-boden* ('The Attic Society', 1946) has a literary programme; it is critical of naturalism and the proletarian novel on the one hand, and on the other of the intervention of philosophy and abstraction (summed up in the word 'Tiefsinn', 'profoundness') in literature. Laurel and Hardy, Charlie Chaplin and Westerns appeal to the members of Kreuder's secret society as more stimulating models; one is reminded here of the juxtaposition of James Joyce and Zane Grey in Graham Greene's *The Third Man*. The society meets in an attic lumber-room with the purpose of combating the stupidity of everyday realism and middle-class conventionality by means of the imagination. They see in the immediate post-war situation justification enough for their attitude of wayward hedonism. *Die Unauffindbaren* ('Those Who cannot be found', 1948) is a longer novel expanding the programme of *Die Gesellschaft vom Dachboden*, which it indicates through an opening quotation from Jean Paul: 'Literature is not a flat mirror of the present, but the magic mirror of a time which does not exist.' An estate-agent leaves his wife and two children one Sunday afternoon just before tea and drifts into a series of adventures involving him in a society of people who defy the claims of the common-sense world. The background of the action is American, but this is only intended as a conventional back-cloth to prevent the reader from seeking props in the common-sense world. The whole action may be the ramblings of a mind which in the delirium of an illness escapes from the ties of reason and responsibility into the liberating fluidity of fantasy, the true fulfilment of the unconscious mind. The gossamer tenuousness and effortless limpidity of Kreuder's prose, its containment of colloquialisms within an enveloping lyricism are qualities that the reader of English will find in Henry Green or L. P. Hartley. *Herein ohne anzuklopfen* ('Come In Without Knocking', 1954) is more explicit than *Die Unauffindbaren* in its approach; the author's criticism of modern life takes the form of a plea for the quiet, contemplative way of the Eastern mystics. Let us throw away our alarm-clocks, leave the roaring stream of traffic on the Autobahn, and liberate ourselves from the twin tyrannies of power-lust and fear. It is more sensible to retire to a private mental home, there to smoke cigarettes, drink Nescafé, gin and bottled beer, and talk, than to be caught up in the hectic routine of modern industrial society. The big three—birth, fate and death—will in any case insist on coming in without knocking. There is a nice spirit of fun and irony to leaven the philosophizing of this novel. We must recapture our lost innocence:

'Something must have got lost at some time, something in us, a sense which once affected us so that things were not as they are now, and that we were all right.'
'Can't we find this sense again?'
'It has not only got lost,' I said, 'I am afraid it has been destroyed and has left us.'
'Who destroyed it?'
'Our thinking,' I said, 'that is, we ourselves. With our thinking we have driven out and destroyed something that is older than ourselves, that is as old as eternity.'
'How do we know about it then?'
'There are still traces of it to be found in the myths and fairy-tales.'
'What is it then?' she asked.
'Innocence,' I said . . .

Somewhat in the manner of Kreuder are the short stories of Kurt Kusenberg (born 1904). They are less ambitious as a criticism of life, and aim first and foremost at being easy and entertaining. Frivolity and fantasy are neatly blended, with an undertone of melancholy which sighs for an escape from the limitations of everyday reality. He has published four volumes of short stories, the two most recent being *Die Sonnenblumen* ('The Sunflowers', 1951) and *Wein auf Lebenszeit* ('Wine for Life', 1955).

Kreuder's surrealism is of a wistful, whimsical gentleness, but other writers who have been attracted to this manner of writing assume a much fiercer and volcanic approach to the subject-matter of their work. Hans Erich Nossack's (born 1901) *Nekyia. Bericht eines Überlebenden* ('Nekyia. Account of a Survivor', 1947) ruthlessly abandons the narrative conventions of place and time, and plunges us into a dream-world which is to symbolize the transition between death and reincarnation, and in addition the interim period of chaos immediately after the collapse of Germany in 1945. As the sole survivor of a dead city, the protagonist questions the relevance of time and memory:

> For what is actually said by the phrase 'There lies something behind me'? Formerly there was nothing more reliable than chronology. Everything was exactly divided and could be expressed in figures. One man was thirty years old and another had been alive a thousand years ago. The calculation was right too, but the basic assumption is no longer the same. Time has been smashed . . .

The narrator is a modern Orestes, and behind any soldier's return from war in or after 1945 stands the archetypal Agamemnon's home-coming from Troy. Nossack's 'Bericht' is so violently opposed to what E. M. Forster, in *Aspects of the Novel*, has called the 'chopped-off length of the tapeworm of time', that it ceases to be a story; the causal thread has gone. The volume *Dorothea* (1948) consists of 'Berichte', as if Nossack were wishing his work to be thought of as reporting, not fiction. A being from another planet who has been sent to observe the situation in Germany writes:

> The day lies behind them [humanity], and knowledge that it was light in vain, makes them sceptical of everything. But how can one expect of beings who have no faith in themselves that they will come through the dark?

The bombing of Hamburg in July 1943 forms the central experience of the book, and is reported in 'Der Untergang'. 'Interview mit dem Tode' relates sardonically conditions in Hamburg in May 1947; death is no longer a reaper, a veiled figure in black or a consumptive young man—he is the black-marketeer who is out and about at night, lies in in the morning, has his room heated in late spring and drinks real coffee. A more recent prose work of Nossack's, *Spätestens im November* ('At Latest in November', 1955), is a more sustained piece of narrative writing than any of the earlier volumes. The outline of its action is simple; the wife of a wealthy industrialist falls in love with a writer whose work is just beginning to find recognition. She leaves her husband and child, lives for a time with the impoverished writer, returns after a few months to her family, but again goes off with her lover to meet death with him when he crashes in his newly acquired second-hand *Volkswagen*. Times have changed since the depression of the immediate post-war years, and Nossack's satire is here directed against the captain of industry with his incessant pre-occupation with the expansion of his factories, the amassing of wealth and power, and his ambition to be respected as a model business-man. He is an easy target for the satirist, and the contrast with the feckless man of letters, to whom he is Maecenas and cuckold, is pointed enough. In its narrative method this novel is less experimental than the earlier works; the events are seen consistently from the woman's point of view, and unfolded with a bare directness of exposition. The division of loyalty between the business world and that of the artist is also the theme of *Der jüngere Bruder* (1958).

Gottfried Benn (1886–1956), mordant and clinical dissector of life from his early Expressionist writings onwards, was primarily a lyrical poet whose sensuous language alternately lures the reader with a seductive fascination or stupefies him into a deep freeze with its intellectual pretentiousness. His '*Berliner Novelle*', *Der Ptolemäer* (1949), has no plot, and consists of the ruminations of a Berlin beauty-specialist (his parlour is significantly called 'Lotos') who looks at life in 1947 with a depressive grittiness. Berlin is a destroyed Carthage now, and the future can promise at most luxury and mundane emptiness; the coming century will only allow, apart from the masses, two types, the criminal and the monk. Life is now cheap; an occasional murder or death in the streets from hunger and cold arouses no interest. What are the achievements of the human mind? Benn's protagonist dismisses the whole scientific outlook from Kepler and Galileo onwards as nugatory, and sees religion as self-deception. He is willing to accept the epithets of nihilist and cynic; art is what matters, he tells us. Against the traditional idea of development of personality, Benn advocates the rights and power of the artist:

Do not perfect your personality, but your separate works. Blow the world as if it were glass, like a breath from a pipe . . . The artist is the only man who can get the better of things and who can make decisions about them. All the other types just go on messing the problems up . . . that is why I said: the glass-blower.

The unreal city behind a vast and concentrated array of literary and philosophical allusions recalls T. S. Eliot's *The Waste Land* or W. H. Auden's *The Age of Anxiety*; Benn in fact wrote a foreword to the German translation of this latter work. With his forceful and elastic style that can absorb jargon and yet remain poetic, Benn became a figure of considerable influence after 1945, purveying a narcotic nihilism that is as consistent an extension of the gloomier potentialities of Nietzsche's thought as we are likely to find anywhere.

Proserpina (1932), the first novel of Elisabeth Langgässer (1899–1950), shows the forces of good and evil fighting for the soul of a five-year-old child; the work is a prose-poem using psycho-analytical and surrealist technique. In short stories dating from the same year, for instance 'Mars', violence and crude realism are uppermost. This author published one further volume of eighteen short stories *Der Torso* ('The Torso', 1947), which reflects moods and episodes in war-time Germany with laconic grimness and flashes of compassionate humour. One cannot help regretting that Elisabeth Langgässer did not give more of her time to this genre and less to the long novel. For her two major works are the post-war novels, *Das unauslöschliche Siegel* ('The Indelible Seal', 1946) and *Märkische Argonautenfahrt* ('Argonauts' Journey in Mark Brandenburg', 1950). *Das unauslöschliche Siegel* analyses, with a fervour that is close to incoherence, the two crises in the life of a Jew who becomes a Roman Catholic; his denial of faith and consequent desertion of his wife and child in 1914, and his spiritual regeneration after his second wife has been murdered in 1925. The period between the two crises is a time when Belfontaine has denied his past, is attempting to live a life of cultured hedonism which shall deny all else but the present moment. It is not only a denial of his personal memory, but also of his national origin; the German who has been interned in France during the first world war marries into French provincial society and is wholly accepted by it. Elisabeth Langgässer's hero loses his way in barren wastes of triviality and despair, to be rescued from a surrealist hell by the miracle of grace. This novel has points in common with her earlier novel *Der Gang durch das Ried* ('The Way Through the Marshland', 1936). Here a Mainz butcher's son, terrified of his unbalanced father's sadistic tendencies, runs away and joins the French Foreign Legion, returning years later, in 1930, to the district of his childhood after being released from a mental home. He is still unbalanced, and tries in vain to fit his childhood memories into his adult personality as a French ex-soldier. *Das unauslöschliche Siegel* is over-diffuse. The retelling of the story of Bernadette of Lourdes may be relevant to Belfontaine's problems, but the long episodes relating Hortense's unrequited love for a man who becomes a priest and her subsequent perverse relationship with the girl Belfontaine is later to marry are linked to the main story only by slight threads. *Märkische Argonauten-fahrt*, less rambling than *Das unauslöschliche Siegel*, portrays a journey made in the summer of 1945 by a group of people from Berlin to a monastery in the Brandenburg country where some of them are to find the golden fleece of divine grace. Salvation is to be found through remembering, not forgetting, through awareness of individual personality, we are told, and through the figure of the ex-soldier Friedrich am Ende is directed the author's criticism of writers such as Kasack or Kreuder whose pantheism offends her. The concluding episode dealing with the corruption of a boy by a gang of black-marketeers reminds us of Graham Greene's underworld, and there are points in common between Greene and Elisabeth Langgässer— their common faith as converts, their portrayal of the innocence and corruptibility of childhood, their preoccupation with sex and sin, with violence and crime, but these two novelists are poles apart in their narrative methods, and Elisabeth Langgässer's complex prose-style and unusual vocabulary are much more ornate than Graham Greene's manner. She handles the interior monologue with a rhapsodical fervour which recalls Faulkner rather than Joyce. Faulkner's *A Fable*, that massive re-creation of Christ as the common soldier whose resistance to the futility of trench warfare in 1914–18 leads to his martyrdom, might well be the novel which Elisabeth Langgässer would have liked to have been able to call her own. The name of Bernanos also comes to mind when one considers Elisabeth Langgässer's sultry and confused vision of humanity caught up in the toils of irrational evil, though vouchsafed awareness of the divine.

Werner Warsinsky's *Kimmerische Fahrt* ('Cimmerian Journey', 1953), a first novel, presents an analysis of a mind that has become deranged by war which recalls Langgässer's *Der Gang durch das Ried*, and a poetically stylized vision of the transition from life to death which has something of the manner of Broch's *Der Tod des Vergil*. Warsinsky succeeds in informing the stream of consciousness structure with colourful language and with a realistic background of the war in Russia and of the broken man's groping for life in post-war Germany, helpless as he is in his search for a reintegrated personality. His journey to the land of constant darkness allows of no safe return to the world of light and normality. This work, like that of Langgässer, suffers from its over-insistent exploitation of the analytic approach to the novel, with the result that an overall impression of subjective confusion remains, in spite of many isolated passages of power.

The world of Heinz Risse (born 1898) has much in common with that of the surrealists, but his style and narrative methods are more traditional. He is no specialist in fine writing, but depicts action with quick-moving, bare lines, and has no fear of a juxtaposition of melodrama and fantasy with everyday realism. He may be called something of a disciple of Kafka. His first novel, *Wenn die Erde bebt* ('The Earthquake', 1950), and its successor, *So frei von Schuld* ('So Free of Guilt', 1951), are symbolist 'philosophical tales' in the sense of Voltaire's *Candide* or *Zadig*, and start out from a hinterland of Calvinist predestination. *Wenn die Erde bebt* has as its central character a man who can foretell the future; it is ironical that someone with such gifts should be employed in an insurance office, where, however, he annoys the management by his refusal to put his services at the firm's disposal. He dislikes what he calls the elephantiasis of capitalism just as much as communism, which he considers its equally materialistic opposite. When the earthquakes come and the fabric of civilization is torn, he is glad, for disaster brings a new spirit of friendship and helpfulness among people. But when order is restored, the old pushing, uncharitable selfishness reasserts itself, and the protagonist is once more the eccentric outsider. *So frei von Schuld* is about a man whom a variety of unmerited disasters befall—a twelve years' sentence for a crime he has not committed, the loss of his only child in a railway accident, his wife's death through illness, the more general confusion through invasion (the country is split in two after being overrun by a military organization that is pledged to the abolition of wealth and religion). The hero's moral idealism is put to the severest tests (we are reminded of the plot situations in the novels of F. M. Klinger, Goethe's friend and contemporary), until finally he wants, like Dostoievsky's Ivan Karamazov, to hand God the ticket back. If his ideal of love and forgiveness is a good thousand years out of date, is there no alternative but a nightmare of crass materialism, the choice of Bazarov in Turgenev's *Father's and Children*? Risse is a moralist who comments on the predicament of modern man in symbolical terms; this he does also in his humorous little insect-fables (*Belohne dich selbst*, 'Take Your Own Reward', 1953). His first novel, showing the earthquakes in their physically and psychologically disintegrating effect on conventional society, reflects the impact of the war on German life, though it is somewhat dubious how far a series of natural calamities may be equated with the man-made disasters of war. *So frei von Schuld* has as its social background the division of Germany into two by occupation forces. *Dann kam der Tag* ('Then the Day Came', 1953) is a criticism of the managerial mentality and the plutocratic conception of success. In *Wenn die Erde bebt* the protagonist has murdered his wife, and is under medical observation; *Dann kam der Tag* has as its central figure a man of seventy, who has attempted to set fire to the factory which he owns. After a life-time of fighting for money and power the old man realizes that he has lost emotional sincerity and moral integrity, and that this is a loss which matters; his belated efforts to make good his past misdeeds are regarded by the outside world as manifestations of senility. The novel is simpler in its action and thought than the first two; it puts moral issues more clearly, but is less interesting as a novel. Although Risse's first story was a *Novelle*, he is more at home in the longer novel. *Irrfahrer* ('Man Adrift', 1948) is the story of a prisoner-of-war and his re-orientation in the peace-time world, while *Simson und die kleinen Leute* ('Samson and the Little People', 1954) is the sad, ironic tale of a poor carrier and his horse. At his best, Risse writes novels of ideas which come to life, overcast with melancholy, but terse and concentrated.

The major work of Hans Henny Jahnn (born 1894) is the novel *Fluß ohne Ufer* ('River Without Banks') which he was writing during his exile on Bornholm from 1933 onwards and of which three volumes have so far appeared. The title indicates the theme: the river of life, or the stream of consciousness, which is a daemonic, elemental force knowing no control. Jahnn's hero learns to identify himself with the raw, teeming life of sailors' quarters in South American and African ports and the bleaker poverty of a Norwegian coastal community. Gustav Anias Horn loses his fiancée when the 'Lais', a ship with a mysterious freight, goes down, and the memory of this catastrophe throws his whole life out of course. He refuses to see his parents again or to assume normal social responsibilities, but in perverse friendship with the man who murdered his fiancée lives first among half-castes and negroes and later in isolation in Norway. A rebel against all traditional usages, he is passionately indignant at the injustice of race and class distinctions. A cultured handful of white folk in America and Europe may be in fact the conscious mind of humanity, but let them beware of their dependence on the inarticulate but vast and vital mass of mankind who are beneath them. If materialism is the right interpretation of the world, all life is equally holy, and if all life is holy, then life's fulfilment in the present should not be distorted by the memory of past failures. It is the paradox of Horn's life that as a man of forty-nine he is haunted by the shadows of the catastrophe that befell the ship

'Lais' twenty-seven years before, although he has so strenuously being trying to live for the moment and to deny the validity of any code that would compel him to assume a responsibility which he resents. *Fluß ohne Ufer* is, like Mann's *Doktor Faustus* and Broch's *Der Tod des Vergil*, in part a 'Künstlerroman', a novel about an artist. Horn gradually realizes his potentialities as a musician and composer (Jahnn refers in an essay *Über den Anlaß* ('Concerning the Cause', 1954) to his admiration for the Danish composer Carl Nielsen); characteristically enough, it is a pianola in a seedy South American hotel that makes the young man thrill to the discovery of a new talent. Jahnn's style is highly individualistic without being obscure or mannered, and his use of imagery is startling and stark. The incident at the opening of the second book of *Die Niederschrift des Gustav Anias Horn* is typical of Jahnn's manner:

I was deeply stirred. I will relate it briefly: I heard out of a heap of loosely piled-up dry pine twigs the beating of the wings of a big insect. I came close and recognized a dragon-fly which was fluttering anxiously in the open lattice-work of the small branches. It was not possible to recognize at once why the creature did not seek freedom, which seemed so easy to attain. The movements of the insect became wilder and more desperate. It pushed against the ground with its head. It did not seem to recognize its surroundings. I bent down and now saw that a number of ants were spraying acid over the dragon-fly's great netted eyes; others were biting with their mandibles into these very eyes. I quickly stepped in to liberate the creature. It was too late. It had already been blinded, or partially blinded. It fell, beating its wings, to earth . . . It died within a minute of over-strain, having succumbed to a heart-attack or to the unimaginable pain of blinding.

The maiming and destruction of the good and beautiful is seen as something horrifying but inevitable. *Fluß ohne Ufer* is nightmarish in quality, for all the plausible realism of its setting. The narrator preserves the body of his dead friend and keeps the coffin as a piece of house-furniture; such wayward surrealist motifs recall episodes in Kreuder and others, but Jahnn outdoes them all in eruptive violence.

IX

THE LENGTH OF TIME

THE preoccupation with time and memory is a characteristic feature of much twentieth-century writing, and in this connection Hermann Broch (1886–1951) is, with his fellow-Austrian contemporaries Musil and Doderer, one of the most important writers in German in this analytical manner. Broch has indicated something of his approach to fiction in his account of the genesis of *Die Schuldlosen* ('The Innocent Ones', 1950), an epilogue where he explains the method of composition of the work and sums up what he considers to be the function of the novel form. The novel, he says, must depict a 'world totality', increasingly difficult though this is as the world becomes more complex and incoherent. This totality must not be on one plane only, since the novelist need not be limited by the naturalist convention, but should include the moral and metaphysical. Can the novel have a social purpose, he asks. Only the converted will be convinced, scepticism may say; but nevertheless the purpose of art is to be moral—it is to be 'Läuterung', purification, and Broch cites Goethe's *Faust*. For Broch the most significant modern writer was James Joyce; he wrote an essay 'James Joyce und die Gegenwart' ('James Joyce and the Present', 1936) in honour of Joyce's fiftieth birthday, and in the epilogue to *Die Schuldlosen* he endowed Leopold Bloom with a representative significance extending well beyond the confines of *Ulysses*. Broch's search for totality of experience is expressed mainly on the social plane in the trilogy *Die Schlafwandler* ('The Sleepwalkers', 1931–2); Pasenow, the Prussian officer, finds in 1918 an affinity with the Social Democratic working man Esch through the common bond of their search for moral principles, but the friendship is destroyed by the unscrupulousness of Hugenau, the calculating materialist who is to inherit the new post-war world. Already the stream of consciousness technique is used in the third volume of the trilogy. The later novel, *Die Schuldlosen*, has resemblances with *Die Schlafwandler*; it too covers three periods of time, 1913–1923–1933, as *Die Schlafwandler* has its three sections, 1888–1903–1918. The earlier novel is more satisfactory in its attempt to give a picture of society in transformation, achieving as it does a broader sweep and at the same time being so highly wrought. *Die Schuldlosen* is an interesting, if uneven experiment. The author has taken a number of his early sketches and tales, written in the first place independently of each other, and has added to them new stories with the aim, imperfectly realized, of bringing the whole into one coherent narrative. This 'novel in eleven stories' is a series of tales which can be taken as separate works, but which are also to be read as consecutive sections of a whole work. Behind the surface reality of the middle-class sphere in which the action is unfolded there looms a complex scaffolding of symbolism in the surrealistic manner.

Der Tod des Vergil ('The Death of Virgil', 1945) is Broch's most difficult and at the same time most homogeneous and distinguished work. This record of the last eighteen hours of Virgil's life is a vast interior monologue that reflects the sensations and thoughts of a highly sensitive and intelligent man who knows that he is dying; the monologue is only interrupted by conversation that the poet himself hears or takes part in. The work covers a whole range of experience, from the crudity of the drunken revellers in the street outside to the most abstract expressions of the poet's quest for truth; it carries within it a wide historical synthesis, and Broch himself has said that the parallels between the first pre-Christian century and our own time are deliberate. On his death-bed the poet wants to destroy the manuscript of his *Aeneid*; art is not enough, and moreover his has been an art that has allowed itself to be subordinated to unworthy ends. In his last hours Virgil sees his own life and its problems in a new light. There is a highly wrought scene between the emperor Augustus and the poet which brings the human issues of the work to a dramatic climax.

For all Broch's conscious affinities to James Joyce in his experimental technique, there is an important difference between the two men. Broch's firm ethical beliefs separate him from Joyce's outlook, as expressed in Stephen Dedalus' 'I will not serve'. There is nothing parodistic in the Salvation Army scenes or in Esch's Bible study in *Die Schlafwandler*; *Die unbekannte Grösse* ('The Unknown Quantity', 1933) preaches the futility of the search for knowledge if this is divorced from the developed heart; Virgil presents his *Aeneid* as a gift to Augustus from motives of loving self-sacrifice, and there is an Old Testament severity behind *Die Schuldlosen*, with its castigation of indifference and of refusal to assume moral and political responsibility.

Broch's posthumously published novel *Der Versucher* ('The Tempter', 1953) is on the broad scale of *Die Schlafwandler* and *Der Tod des Vergil*, and like them it is more convincing than the somewhat cerebral and abstract *Die Schuldlosen*. It is a peasant novel set in an Austrian Alpine community, and its action may be assumed to take place during the period when the author was first working on it, the years 1934–6. Although the final form of the novel had not been completed when Broch died, the work has been edited as a convincing whole by patient reference to the various versions that are in existence. What is surprising is that after *Der Tod des Vergil* and *Die Schuldlosen* Broch went on to make more use of traditional narrative methods, and this last novel shows clearly his control over action, suspense and characters conceived in these terms. A remote and largely primitive village populace succumbs to the oratory of a vagrant fanatic; in an uprush of mass hysteria this man's influence reaches its height in the committing of a ritual murder. The action is seen through the eyes of the village doctor, a middle-aged man who has forsaken eminence in the city for the obscurity of general practice in this out-of-the-way spot; he is a complex figure, one of the community of rough peasants and their familiar confidant, and yet separated from them by his work and his background. As a three-dimensional novel of village life *Der Versucher* has something of the vitality and grandeur of Jeremias Gotthelf's narratives of Bernese peasant life

—in particular, the theme of healing recalls the issues of the Swiss author's *Anne Bäbi Jowäger*; however, Gotthelf's peasant families have a norm of Christian belief which is lacking here, for the weakness of the Church's influence in this village is one of the factors which permit the tempter to lead it astray. Broch combines straightforward narrative with visions and monologues indicative of primitive, tellurian forces. His protagonist says:

> Our life is dreaming and waking at once, and if the chill wind of dreams occasionally blows into that world which we call reality—and it does so more often than we think—, this reality becomes sometimes strangely illuminated and deep like a landscape after a cool shower of rain, or like speech which all at once is no longer a mere string of words telling of things that have happened in some shapeless limbo, but which has been breathed upon by a higher reality and has suddenly gained the power to portray things as they are with life and warmth.

The rhapsodic evocation of subconscious perspectives of symbolic depth does not wholly blend with the straightforward depiction of people and action in terms of common-sense realism. The different layers of perception remain disparate, so that the problem of combining them in an artistic whole is still unsolved. This last novel of Broch's is nevertheless fascinating and powerful.

Robert Musil's (1880–1942) vast 1,600-page novel *Der Mann Ohne Eigenschaften* ('The Man Without Qualities') was left in an unfinished state at his death in Geneva and was first made available in its entirety in Germany in 1952. Although chronologically, therefore, it was composed at an earlier period, its influence on contemporary German readers has only begun recently. The publication of the first part in 1930 gained its author a *succès d'estime*, but during the years of his exile in Switzerland Musil was virtually a forgotten man. His first novel, one of the pioneer works anticipating the Expressionist movement, had been his most successful; *Die Verwirrungen des Zöglings Törleß* ('The Confusions of Schoolboy Törless', 1906) is a harsh story of sexual perversion and brutality in a boarding school. *Der Mann ohne Eigenschaften* is vast, monumental and stuffed with encyclopaedic learning; it is comparable to some work of Thomas Mann or Broch, though, if anything, even more formidable reading than *Der Tod des Vergil*. Musil is attempting to embrace the whole predicament of twentieth-century man, as he sees it, and his hero Ulrich is a modern Faust, a man 'without qualities', that is, roughly, without social or ideological commitments. Ulrich looks at Viennese society during the year or so before the outbreak of war in 1914, and sees everywhere uncertain groping for something to believe or else what he considers a smug and dangerous affirmation of values which he finds at best partial solutions. Ulrich stand with ironical reserve apart from the organization, to which he acts as secretary, which is attempting unsuccessfully to find meaning and shape to a proposed 'Austrian Year' to celebrate the seventieth anniversary of the reign of Franz Josef II in 1918. If Ulrich represents the intellect which refuses to content itself until it receives a final answer through reason, the other characters embody allegorically various qualities of which Ulrich and his author disapprove. Arnheim, the son of a Prussian heavy industrialist, is torn between the cultured idealism of German classicism and the demands of practical business life. Diotima, hostess and enthusiast for the 'soul', finds her concern for idealistic synthesis replaced by a desire to study sex-problems. Clarisse is a hysterical young woman whose discontent with marriage to a well-meaning dilettante leads to an obsession with a psychopathic murderer, Moosbrugger, whom she assists to escape from gaol; she would like to become the living reconciliation of Nietzsche and Christ, but after the escaped Moosbrugger kills yet another victim, she becomes completely unbalanced mentally. If the first sections of the novel are social comedy, always intellectually demanding and sometimes sparklingly witty, the later sections become increasingly gloomy and increasingly clogged up with dissertation at the expense of action or psychological analysis. The form which Ulrich's search for truth takes in the latter half of the work is incredible from the point of view of his earlier character, and seriously undermines the reader's hope that the hero might be an adequate symbol for Musil's new way of life. In his urge to break with conventional morality and seek what he hopes will be a more real and modern code, he is an accomplice with his sister in the forging of their father's will. Brother and sister later have an incestuous relationship on a visit to Italy that is a flight from normal society and a search for new truth. Parallel with this honeymoon with his sister goes Ulrich's study of the mystics, whose feelings and experiences he would like to share, though he would prefer them divorced from religious belief. Ulrich's relationship with Agathe terminates in failure; this was a last attempt to find paradise on a Romantic basis, and they then separate. Back in Vienna, the sketches of the final scenes show the collapse of the campaign for the Austrian Year in the breakdown of the old order with the advent of war. Perhaps Musil intended his work to contain a positive message to the effect that an ascetic search for truth through reason and insight might lead to man's final salvation; but the general tenor of the second half of the book does little to encourage this thought.

The Austrian society which Musil portrays is limited to the well-off intelligentsia, and these too are depicted largely as types, for the author has little interest in realistic detail or in giving a historical picture of pre-1914 Vienna. He dislikes the racialists whose theories anticipated Hitler, and seems to dislike Christianity to much the same degree; Hans Sepp, the young man who opposes the Austrian Year because it is neither anti-Semitic nor specifically pro-German, is shown as having at the same time Christian sympathies while pursuing a love affair with a Jewess. Lindner, a teacher who intervenes when he imagines that Agathe is on the verge of committing suicide, is described sarcastically as a pedantic and bullying representative of the old Christian and Weimar-classical morality. Feuermaul, a poet with internationalist ideals who is in part a caricature of Werfel, is another butt for Musil's sarcasm. In his opposition to traditional morality Musil's hero is echoing the tortured questionings of Ivan in Dostoievsky's *The Brothers Karamazov*, and he turns inside out the commandment to love one's neighbour as oneself, much as Gide and Rilke pulled to pieces the parable of the prodigal son. Nietzsche and

Freud stand in the background as fairy-godmothers to Musil's conception of man and society.

Apart from his sister, there are two or perhaps three people whose ideas Ulrich takes seriously. The nymphomaniac Bonadea embodies the notion of uncommitted promiscuity, and tolerates any other aspects of life with indifferent scepticism. Count Leinsdorf, president of the Collateral Campaign, symbolizes the old order in Austria, a combination of civilized capitalism with the old feudal order; but as disaster approaches, he loses control of the Campaign, and finally his age renders him incapable of grasping the issues any more. Ulrich, like his creator, is interested in mathematics and militarism. The character who is his frequent interlocutor and for whom he develops a strong affection is General Stumm von Bordwehr, the officer responsible for the army's participation in the Collateral Campaign. Stumm is introduced as a seeker after new knowledge, dashed by the unfamiliar immensity of a scholarly library, but not yet daunted, who finds in Ulrich's dry scepticism an outlook which he feels to be more suited to his cast of mind than the sweeping generalizations of Arnheim. All the new intellectual problems which he encounters in the course of his activity on behalf of the Austrian Year are referred to military precedent for his own satisfaction. The outbreak of war brings the army into the forefront of power; but the army can offer no leadership, it wishes only to be an efficiently obedient machine.

From the time of the Weimar Republic onwards Thomas Mann committed his rationalism to social democracy, but Musil's more abstruse scepticism led him to an impatient and intolerant disparagement of Christianity, democracy, international ideals or revolution. His diaries show his confusion and hesitation of mind at the coming to power of the Nazis in 1933; but demagogic totalitarianism soon revealed itself as a travesty of the militaristic nationalism which had appealed to him after 1918. Finding no positive all-embracing solution to social and metaphysical problems, Ulrich is left at the end clinging to the vestiges of an order which he recognizes as bankrupt—a society with a feudal, officer-class hierarchy. With Musil, as with Jünger and Doderer, intellectual scepticism is linked with right-wing traditionalism.

In his best short story, 'Die Portugiesin' ('The Portuguese Woman', from *Drei Frauen*, 1923), Musil tells how a man finds confidence in himself and his wife's fidelity and a will to live by scaling a dangerous cliff-face. Musil's long novel is an undertaking of comparable immensity. 'Thomas Mann and those like him write for people who exist; I write for people who do not!' he wrote in his diary. The novel in the past has been like a sick man talking to his doctor, he says; why should it not be like doctors talking amongst themselves, or at least like a doctor explaining the illness to the patient? The task of the modern writer, he says, is truth, not realism, and he understands by this, it seems, a conception that the novel is not a description of what 'is' but of what 'could be'. Typically Austrian feelings of transience lead Musil to the preoccupation with time and memory, and a consciousness that even if only one set of events do happen, a multitude of alternative possibilities might happen, or might have happened. If Ulrich's reflections are at times witty, they can become tiresomely erudite and abstract. Kafka found an original and striking way of giving expression to his feelings of insecurity and simultaneity, but Musil lacks Kafka's immediacy of vision. He writes meticulously and often penetratingly, but as the novel moves on, what narrative tension there was in the earlier sections becomes further slowed down by the increasing weight of extraneous material, and social comedy is over-shadowed by perversity and gloom. Ulrich is looking for a new morality which is to embrace mathematics and mysticism and to overthrow traditional values; it is a desperate quest, and the conclusion of the novel gives little indication that the hero has come anywhere near the top of his particular cliff-face.

Heimito von Doderer (born 1896), the third of these Austrian monumentalists, has more affinities in his work with Musil than with Broch. In an autobiographical sketch, appended to the story *Das letzte Abenteuer* ('The Last Adventure', 1953), he refers to himself as profoundly disillusioned, capable of surprise at nothing after living through the collapse of four régimes, the Austro-Hungarian monarchy and the Russian czardom, the first Austrian republic, the dictatorships of Dollfuß in Vienna and of the Kolchaks in Siberia. The world of his important work is Viennese society, both during the last years of the old empire and, in fuller detail, the nineteen-twenties. Less interested in philosophical speculation than Musil or Broch, Doderer describes peoples and places with minute care and virtuoso skill; consequently his work is less abstract and subjective, and makes an impression of photographic accuracy over a wide field of vision that is amazing. He denies any wish to write either a historical novel or a documentary *Zeitroman* or *roman fleuve*, though he describes himself, with various qualifications, as a naturalist in his approach to the technique of the novel. His definition of imaginative writing, first formulated in French, has echoes of Proust's methods of rediscovering lost time: 'Ecrire, c'est la grammaire, révélée par un souvenir en choc.' What he is interested in all the time is people. He has a message to deliver, admittedly, and it is roughly the one already familiar to us from Musil, Jünger and others: that we have lost the individuality and strength of the pre-1914 world, and that values in contemporary life have been jettisoned with the advent of mass living, represented by dictatorships of the extreme right or left and by mechanization generally. But in Doderer's novels such general issues are peripheral to his art, for nothing fascinates him more than the daily, hourly miracle of contact between people. A walk in the streets of Vienna, a visit to a café, a party, a telephone call, a visit to a library, a general strike, indeed any means of bringing people together is the wonder which makes the novelist catch his breath with delighted astonishment. Plot and dialogue, accompanied by a commentary that is polished, fanciful, clever and witty, are the essential factors of his narrative. Doderer may possibly have intended his *Die Dämonen* ('The Demons', 1956) to be a solemn warning that life has never been the same since the Palace of Justice in Vienna was burnt down on 15 July 1927, but this novel, with about thirty main characters and a host of subsidiary figures, is above all comedy. Although a certain number of sad happenings take place, for the most part all ends well in a profusion of happy marriages. Only in the case of one of the main characters can we speak of tragedy; Imre von Gyurkicz, a Hungarian adventurer, is shot while speaking in support of a revolutionary cause in which he has little faith, except the negative faith that it is opposed to a fascism he dislikes. In the second half of the novel Gyurkicz, who has tried so hard to become accepted by *Die Unsrigen*, the 'right' people, acquires a belated and lonely grandeur (one thinks of Turgenev's Rudin) as misfortunes assail him.

Die Dämonen overlaps in part with the earlier novel *Die Strudlhofstiege* ('The Strudlhof Steps', 1951), which acts as its prelude. Here the map of Doderer's Vienna is drawn, the full details of which are to be filled in later. A number of the characters appear in both novels, and the principal link is René von Stangeler, whose amorous exploits as a young man in *Die Strudlhofstiege* form the complex prelude to the relative stability of the research historian of *Die Dämonen*. Each of these novels is a separate unit, with its own plot and design; at the same time, for full comprehension of what is happening, it is necessary to read both, for the two novels together form a larger and more complete pattern of incident and characters than either book taken separately. The method of *Die Strudlhofstiege* is to alternate between two sets of incidents, the one period being 1910–13, the other being the summer of 1925. There is a welter of plot, characters, love-affairs and business propositions. Major Melzer, a quiet and unpretentious man, is by social class part of the sophisticated set that teem through these pages, but by nature he is too good for them. As an army officer before the first world war his most memorable experience was bear-hunting in Bosnia, but his shyness prevents him from achieving success in love. After 1918 he is on the rocks for a time, has contact with Eulenfeld, a hard-drinking, whoring and boastful ex-officer, but is thankful to find a niche in the administration of the tobacco-tax department. Melzer is the *Bildungsroman* type of the retiring, introspective and ordinary individual who has a long struggle before he gains self-confidence and social integration. But *Die Strudlhofstiege* is more than a *Bildungsroman,* for Melzer's development is, as it were, the string that fastens together a bunch of sub-plots.

Most novels which are concerned with the rehabilitation of lost memories are slow-moving and replace dramatic incident by analysis and a broad delineation of associations of ideas. Doderer takes his time too, but is self-disciplined in his combination of a loving lingering on half-forgotten impressions with a cunning deployment of many characters and plots. He is a juggler who gives no sense of strain or hurry. Inventiveness of plot-devices accompanies him all the time. There are queer dodges and situations, and no scorn for the use of mystifications which were the stock-in-trade of the eighteenth-century novelist; much of the narrative suspense in *Die Strudlhosftiege* is upheld by the presence of identical twins. In *Die Dämonen* the web of intrigue is built round a foundling child, Charlotte (Quapp) von Schlaggenberg, who has to learn that Kajetan is not her brother and that a fortune of 10,000,000 shillings is at stake; Quapp's identity is a matter which sets the big banks rocking, and here again it is the persistent integrity of a middle-aged bachelor who is slow in affairs of the heart, this time Geyrenhoff, which unravels the embroilment in the nick of time. Doderer's virtuosity extends from stylistic detail to fearsomely complicated overall plot-mechanisms; it is to some degree reminiscent of the manner of Jean Paul or Raabe.

Die Strudlhofstiege is Rococo comedy where the slickness of much of the plot is off-set by the more contemplative role of Melzer, who is a 'difficult man' in the sense of Hofmannsthal's comedy *Der Schwierige* as well as a *Bildungsroman* figure. *Die Dämonen* uses the manner of Rococo comedy for a Neo-Gothic theme; the earlier novel is concerned with memory and the private life, though the business intrigue of the immediate post-inflation years anticipates the wider scope of the second novel. In one respect *Die Dämonen* is simpler than *Die Strudlhofstiege*; its action takes over where *Die Strudlhofstiege* left off, on 21 September 1925, when Mary K. lost her leg, and moves steadily forward to its climax of the general strike and the burning of the Palace of Justice, the principal action taking place in the nine months preceding this incident. Doderer is scrupulously fair—indeed, he stands need to be—about the timing, dating and placing of his characters' movements. The device of the 'chronicle' is playful and at times irritating. The main narrator is Geyrenhoff, who has just retired in middle age from the civil service and who begins writing up the story in the spring of 1927 and has it finally ready in 1955. The narrative is at times, it seems, in the hands of Schlaggenberg, a professional novelist, and the two chroniclers make occasional playfully barbed comments on each other's style and interpretation of the events; other interpolations are the 'night-diary' of Frau Kapsreiter, the 'chronique scandaleuse' of Schlaggenberg's would-be scientific investigation of fat ladies (which Geyrenhoff claims to have censored heavily) and a long manuscript concerning the highly irregular detainment of two respectable middle-aged women on a trumped-up charge of witchcraft in the late fourteenth century (this manuscript is reproduced in Early New High German!).

Who and what are the demons? The title clearly harks back to Dostoievsky and to the Gospel story of the Gadarene swine possessed of the devil and hurtling to destruction. European civilization, it seems, has never been the same since 1914, and events in Vienna in 1927 marked the end of an era and were a foreboding, for those who had ears to hear, of the disasters and quick changes that have befallen us since then. The daemonic element in man and society is a constant threat to decency and civilization; the disreputable urges of a sick mind (and Doderer shows all his characters as subject to some degree to such sickness; it is, he assumes, the human condition) undermine the mental health of the individual, while, on the level of the community as a whole, the international financial crooks at the top and at the bottom the criminal underworld of murderers, sneak-thieves, card-sharpers, prostitutes and political spies exploit and aggravate an uneasy political situation for their own low ends. Imre von Gyurkicz and Géza von Orkay, both sympathetic characters, detach themselves from the tentacles of Hungarian fascism, but Eulenfeld and Körger, after the crisis of 15 July 1927, darkly and drunkenly look forward to the advent of such a régime in Austria. The tragedy of the workers' demonstrations of 15 July, as Doderer sees it, is that police and workers were pitted against one another, while in their fundamental decency and integrity they should have been allies against the anti-social forces which were threatening to get the upper hand. In private life the underworld of the unconscious mind breaks through most visibly in a degradation and perversion of sexual instincts.

But Doderer's optimism and sense of comedy win through, in spite of his apparent intentions to present us with a twentieth-century equivalent of Dostoievsky's Cassandra-like warnings to Europe. The central chapter of the novel, 'Dort unten' ('down below'), describes a man's temporary temptation to abuse the machinery of witchcraft trials; this might well have been a gruesome episode, but instead it transpires to be comedy, though of a scurrilous and rather questionable nature. Similarly the social unrest of July 1927, although seen from the public point of view as the 'Cannae of Austrian freedom', still give to the reader on the whole a sense of comedy. For the strike and the fire intervene in the lives of many of the characters with the effect of propelling them into each other's arms and leaving them happy for quite a long time after. The 'demons' may increasingly threaten the future of Austrian society, but the individual characters mostly end up cleared of their private obsessions, inhibitions and quirks.

Doderer talks of a second reality, the world of illusion, fantasy and imagination, which he regards as the inevitable breeding-ground of his demons. With large self-assurance he maintains that there is only one reality, everyday life: 'There is only everyday life, there is absolutely nothing apart from this; it is here and now that one must prove one's worth.' If twentieth-century life cannot accept this point of view, it is, he alleges, subject to degeneracy and confusion. Man must live with resolute extra-version, self-consciously unself-conscious; the second reality, if allowed to lose its rightful subordination to the first reality of common sense, will get out of hand, and society as a whole will be subjected to the doctrinaire illusions of a fanatical dictator, while the individual will lose his mental balance. Much of the novel is concerned with the tracing of this uneasy relationship of illusion and reality, as it affects the different characters. The integration of imagination and practical realism are essential and desirable for happiness; but they are, needless to say, seldom attained, and their alternation forms the drama of life, and, we are told, 'Life means communication, contact, interval between contents. Interval is naturally pain. Pain is the psychic appearance of intervals . . .'

Doderer's novel is not only comedy in the sense of high comedy, but contains numerous funny incidents. Its level is in general less riotous than that of Mann's *Felix Krull*, but there are a number of knock-about scenes. *Die Strudlhofstiege* and *Die Dämonen* are impressive for various reasons, but primarily as a picture of a world which is enormous in its range, extending to many varied aspects of society, and yet built up step by step with elaborate, detailed care as to style, plot, characterization and background. An astonishing combination of patience and self-confidence must have been necessary for the successful completion of this vast work. It is one of the most outstanding and distinguished modern German novels of this century to date.

X

NOVEL AND SHORT STORY

RECENT novelists who have favoured the large-scale, monumental novel have nearly always been practitioners who belong to the generation which was adult in the nineteen-twenties and looked towards Joyce, Proust and their contemporaries as models. If the 'experimental' novel of forty years ago has long since ceased to be a novelty in this country, it has made a renewed appeal in Germany since 1945, in part because German authors who had been frustrated of foreign influences during the Nazi period were eager to make up for lost time by emulating the analytical and often esoteric novels of the nineteen-twenties. Younger authors who have come to writing since 1945 have up to now been more reluctant to embark on books of vast dimensions. Writing has for them not been based on a calculation that twenty or thirty years will be at their disposal for the perfecting of a great work. There may be only one year or one week to write in; and so a novel will seldom be more than 100,000 words long, and the short story will be chosen more frequently as being more rewarding of immediate effect and a more suitable vehicle for the expression of the mood of the moment in a social situation that is changing rapidly. This chapter, while reviewing novels as well as shorter prose fiction by a number of recent authors, will have to give more emphasis to the short story than earlier sections, for this genre figures more extensively in their work.

To what extent are we justified in referring to the short story as an independent literary form in Germany, it may be asked. And are we not accustomed to thinking in terms of novel (*Roman*) and novella (*Novelle*) as predominant narrative forms during the nineteenth century? This is indeed the case, and the novel certainly continues to flourish, though the traditional *Novelle* is being

placed in a somewhat defensive position by the growing popularity of the short story. There are still some signs of uncertainty
among German critics concerning the differentiation of *Novelle*
from short story (*Kurzgeschichte*), though it is now usually
admitted by the critics that the short story has matured to a
reputable literary form in Germany. The authors are usually less
concerned with the critics' definitions of what constitutes a short
story, and they are not inhibited thereby from writing what they
mostly call *Geschichten* and *Erzählungen* of between 1,000 and
6,000 words.

Isolated examples of short stories can be found early in the
nineteenth century in the work of E. T. A. Hoffmann and possibly
Kleist, and certainly in the calendar stories of J. P. Hebel and
Gotthelf. In the mid-nineteenth century and later the *Novelle*
remained the dominant vehicle for shorter narrative fiction, and
claims have been made that a new genre, the sketch (*Skizze*),
came into German literature during the Naturalist period. As
this movement verged into impressionism, the sketch could
become lyrical, the fixing in words of mood and atmosphere
rather than external description. Some of Thomas Mann's early
so-called *Novellen*, such as 'Das Wunderkind' or 'Enttäuschung',
are on the borderline of sketch and story. The sketch was Walser's
favourite form, and Kafka's cameos of Prague life are in this
tradition. Fable and parable come into their own once more in
Kafka's work. There are parallels with stories in the tradition of
the poetic sketch in James Joyce's *Dubliners* and Virginia Woolf's
'Kew Gardens'. In the twentieth century the short story as a
concentrated form of *Novelle*, often called the *Anekdote*, was
frequently practised by authors who consciously dissociated themselves from the manner of the impressionists. Paul Ernst's *Geschichten von deutscher Art* ('Stories in the German Manner', 1928) and
other collections of his short stories exemplify this; Wilhelm
Schäfer's *Anekdoten*, published in various collections between
1907 and 1950, are short stories in length, usually with a historical
background and an emphasis on dramatic action at the expense
of description and psychological analysis. Putting it very generally

and simply, there were in Germany before 1945 two principal streams of short-story writing, the poetic-impressionistic type, often associated with experimental writing, and the plot-centred dramatic type. These already existing traditions were stimulated after 1945 by renewed acquaintance with English and American authors, and perhaps Hemingway has been the most influential figure among these. The most recent German short-story writers prefer contemporary, everyday themes, and there is an increasing predilection for the poetic-impressionistic approach, often combined with wit and fantasy.

The first important volumes of post-war short stories were Elisabeth Langgässer's *Der Torso* and the collected works of Wolfgang Borchert. Brecht's *Kalendergeschichten* were an interesting but isolated revival of a much earlier literary manner. Wolfgang Borchert (1921–47) writes with sensitivity, but without nostalgic regrets for a gentler world that is no longer there; indeed, how could he, since the memory of him and his generation could scarcely recall any time when Germany was not in a state of crisis or confusion. Borchert's style has a quick, febrile quality; it takes colloquialisms and gives them poetic significance; it uses bold images. Apart from a play *Draußen vor der Tür* ('The Man Outside'), Borchert's work consists of short stories and sketches where plot is a secondary consideration, for each tale is held together by style and mood. The sketches 'Im Schnee, im sauberen Schnee' ('In the snow, in the clean snow') reflect the bleak hopelessness of Borchert's experience of the Russian campaign. The story 'Die Hundeblume' relates an episode from prison life; vivid naturalism of description is broken up by the fantastic obsessions of the prisoners in the exercise yard and by the yearning and triumph of the protagonist's desire to possess a dandelion growing there. Borchert is above all else the poet of his native city Hamburg. For all his programmatic nihilism, he is in love with life, and life means the big city and the Elbe:

That is the smell of life! Nappies, cabbage, plush sofa, onions, petrol, girls' dreams, glue, substitute coffee, cats, geraniums, Schnaps, motor tyres, lipstick.

Less sketchy than most of Borchert's short stories is 'Bilbrook', which tells of a young Canadian airman who, arriving in Hamburg for the first time, finds that there is a district which has his name, Bill Brook. But after setting off gaily to visit it, he finds miles and miles of desolation and rubble, and is overwhelmed with terror at a reality that is so unexpectedly frightening. Borchert's disillusioned writing catches the mood of the grim inertia of German life immediately after the end of the war in prose poems of dispassionate sensitivity.

Ilse Aichinger, who was born in 1921 in Vienna, follows the Surrealists. Her first publication was the novel *Die größere Hoffnung* ('The Greater Hope', 1948), which relates in lyrical, stylized manner the fate of a partly Jewish girl from the time when, as an eight-year-old child, she is separated from her mother who has to flee before the German invaders of Austria in 1938, to the day near the end of the war when she meets her death from a stray shot during the street-fighting in Vienna in 1945. There is much that is poignant in this novel—the group of little waifs who have nowhere to play together except the dilapidated Jewish cemetery, or the description of the forced labour conditions in a wartime factory. Ilse Aichinger has achieved a greater formal precision in her collection of short stories *Der Gefesselte* ('The Bound Man', 1953), with their imaginative treatment of the symbolic content of a world underlying the reality of everyday life.

Eine Stimme hebt an ('A Voice is raised', 1950), by Gerd Gaiser (born 1908), is about a home-coming soldier who is not so much disillusioned as benumbed by the war and what has followed from it. His wife has been unfaithful to him, and he prefers to go back to the country town where he spent his boyhood. For a time his wounded spirit is silent and unresponsive; but in the chaotic years of 1946 and 1947 he gradually regains a constructive outlook on life. In an atmosphere of bewilderment, apathy and corruption it is shown how a few people are still capable of heroic self-sacrifice or unspectacular devotion to everyday duties. There are many good descriptions of the living conditions of this time; particularly vivid is that of the townspeople trekking into the countryside to beg, barter or steal the damson crop in the summer heat. The style recalls the manner of Elisabeth Langgässer; with all its striking qualities it is over-complex, and the blurring of surface reality with archetypal symbols sometimes leads to obscurity. Gaiser's second novel, *Die sterbende Jagd* ('The Dying Squad', 1953; translated into English as 'The Falling Leaf'), is more sombre and humanly less interesting than *Eine Stimme hebt an*. The action takes place within one week, and shows how German fighter-pilots stationed in Norway came to realize that their task of resisting the attacking squadrons from Great Britain is an impossible one because of the fewness of their numbers and the inferiority of their machines; how too it now becomes fully clear to them that the cause for which they have been fighting is an unworthy one, and that the whole premises of their actions are in consequence false. Although the style of this work is more direct and realistic than that of *Eine Stimme hebt an*, the predominance of *Luftwaffe* slang and jargon makes it heavy reading for the uninitiated, while the diffusion of the interest over a large number of isolated characters leads to a certain incoherence in the narrative. *Das Schiff im Berg* ('The Ship in the Mountain', 1953) in some ways recalls the theme of Broch's *Der Versucher*. A poor community living on a mountain side discover that the mountain is tunnelled through with forgotten caves which, it is now hoped, will bring prosperity in the form of tourist trade. The hero of the book is the mountain itself, whose development from primitive times onwards is told in flashbacks; the mountain is myth and pre-history as well as a contemporary phenomenon to be exploited for commercial purposes.

Gaiser's novels to date are less memorable than his short stories collected in the volume *Einmal und oft* ('Once and Often', 1957). 'Gianna aus dem Schatten' ('Gianna from the Shadows'), the longest tale in this volume, describes the retribution that befalls a man who on a visit to Italy as a tourist chances to meet again a woman who, as a partisan in the resistance movement during the war, has an old score to settle with this German ex-soldier. He is driven as if inevitably into a situation which exposes him to her power; but in the immediate reaction of grief which assails her after she has shot him, the wronged woman discovers that the repayment of wrong by revenge has brought no satisfaction, only arid emptiness. Gaiser sometimes makes use of the interior monologue, and overlays everyday reality with symbolism, with considerable effect in the short story 'Ich warte auf Ness' ('I am waiting for Ness'); here a man recalls how a girl companion once saved him as a twelve-year-old boy from drowning in an icy pool, and how this episode, pushed into the background of his mind for many years, comes to be the one meaningful centre in his life. Gaiser's characters, for instance the narrator of 'Vorspiel' ('Prelude'), suffers from the realization of the presence of so much evil in the world, both in man and nature, but are buoyed up by the conviction of the reality of goodness as revealed in the strong instinct to sympathize and help which human beings show.

Hans Bender (born 1919) returned from Russia in 1949, where he had been a prisoner-of-war, and he writes poetry and fiction with a cool, lyrical approach. The title of his volume of collected short stories, *Wölfe und Tauben* ('Wolves and Doves', 1957), indicates something of his attitude to his characters, who are seen as wolves or doves, aggressive or suffering, cruel or fearful. He is careful to give the appearance that he is the factual recorder of moods and impressions picked up with apparent casualness and described with delicacy and punctiliousness of language. The stories reflecting experiences in Russia and afterwards avoid direct statement of attitude or value-judgement, but depict limited horizons and psychological reactions. A German officer deceives a Russian woman about the possibility of securing her son's return home and is then shot by partisans. Or a shepherd in a German village cannot bring himself to slaughter his sheep, as he has been ordered by American occupation authority. 'Die Wölfe kommen zurück' ('The Wolves come back') tells of some German prisoners-of-war during the first days of their life under the charge of the Starost of a remote Russian village. The Russian's rifle is revealed to be useless—there is no ammunition—either for guarding prisoners or for shooting at packs of predatory wolves. But the return of the wolves from the East is an indication that the war is over, and that Germans and Russians can live together here without weapons between them. Although not directly forceful, these tales have their own quiet fascination. Heinz Albers (born 1925), in a volume of short stories *Landung ohne Ankunft* ('Landing Without Arrival', 1957), writes frequently about the sea, and acknowledges Joseph Conrad as an author whose work he greatly admires. Albers aims to write with validity and precision, to tell a story directly, but at the same time to illuminate the inner life by poetry. Herbert Eisenreich (born 1925), an Austrian writer, has written in *Böse schöne Welt* ('Wicked, Beautiful World', 1957) unsparing analyses in the experimental manner of emotional crises. He is an advocate of the short story as a form of prose lyric, and would no doubt approve of Elizabeth Bowen's words: 'Amazement—involuntary and to a degree fathomed—is part of poetry. In the short story, semi-poetic, amazement is not only not fathomed but not stated; but has to be made evident' (*The Faber Book of Modern Short Stories*, edited by Elizabeth Bowen, 1936).

Satirical wit, sharp and delicate, linked with surrealist fantasy give the work of Wolfdietrich Schnurre (born 1920) and Wolfgang Hildesheimer (born 1916) a peculiar precision. *Sternstaub und Sänfte* ('Stardust and Sedan-Chair', 1953) breaks down attempts to classify it normally. This diary of a canine Felix Krull, a sonnet-writing poodle, sometimes seems to be almost a novel, though more often a collection of aphorisms and jokes; it is spare, dry and satirical. Hildesheimer's short stories, such as 'Ich trage eine Eule nach Athen' ('I Carry an Owl to Athens', that is, 'coals to Newcastle', 1956), are amusing in a similar vein, entertaining because of their neat expression of not quite total absurdity. The collection of short stories *So zärtlich war Suleyken* ('Suleyken was so Charming', 1955), by Siegfried Lenz, conjures up village and farm life in a remote part of East Prussia as it may have been before 1939. The author is continuing the older tradition of regionalism—one is reminded, for instance, of Hermann Sudermann's *Litauische Geschichten* ('Lithuanian Stories', 1917)—but with an admixture of the particular wit and polish that are cultivated by Schnurre or Hildesheimer. 'Reality is a task . . . It requires our active, not our passive attention. What is real *is* fantastic.' These words of Heinrich Böll (born 1917) reveal his consciousness of the problem which has beset so many modern German novelists. The reality which Böll describes is closer to the life of his German contemporaries than the *fin de siècle* refinement of the Neo-Romantics. What came before 1939 belongs to a past before the deluge, and plays only a small part in his imaginative world. After the war comes the peace; Böll recalls the chaos and the starvation amid the ruined towns, the advent of the currency reform, bringing neon-lights and shop-windows for all, and hot sausages and coffee too, if one can spare a Mark or so, and the new generation which is growing up with no conscious memory of the war and which takes for granted the cream-cakes and *Volkswagen*. But for Böll the present has been conditioned by the trauma of the years 1939–45.

His first two novels deal directly with war experiences. *Der Zug war pünktlich* ('The Train was on Time', 1949) recounts the brief days in a soldier's life in 1943 from the time when he boards a special train in the Ruhr in order to be transported back to the Eastern front. *Wo warst du, Adam* ('Where were you, Adam', 1950) narrates the fate of a group of officers and men who are retreating from Rumania to Germany in 1945. By comparison with Böll's subsequent writing, the characters and situations in these two novels are too black and white, and the starkness is exaggerated. The conception of reality as a task or duty leads to a consideration of the novelist as moralist. Böll's two novels of family life illustrate this aspect of his writing: *Und sagte kein einziges Wort* (English translation, 'Acquainted with the Night', 1953) and *Haus ohne Hüter* ('House without a Guardian', 1954). All his fiction is firmly fixed in its social background, and different works satirize or expose various evils of contemporary society, with something of the programmatic approach of Diderot in the *drame bourgeois* or Brecht in his epic theatre; a comparison with Dickens might also be made. Böll's early novels show the isolation of the little man who is exposed to the sufferings and evils brought about by war and the post-war situation. The specific problem of *Und sagte kein einziges Wort* is the threat to family life of un-satisfactory living situations; a man and his wife have been living with their three children for eight years in a single room. It is the wife who suffers in silence, contends with the grim chores (the bomb-damaged walls shower dust and dirt continuously), struggles to bring up the children and to manage the neuroses of her husband, a man who has never made any serious attempt to conform with conventional respectability. Behind the bustlingly efficient ambitiousness of German economic recovery he sees emptiness and horror. For the husband in this novel life can have no meaning unless the sting of death is removed. 'Do you believe in the resurrection of the dead?' he asks a priest. *Haus ohne Hüter* is less clear-cut than *Und sagte kein einziges Wort*. Much of this novel is seen from the point of view of a couple of eleven-year-old boys who have never known their fathers. Each child recog-nizes that there is something lacking about his mother; Martin has wealth around him (the family have an interest in a jam factory), but his mother's emotional life has become arrested in a Hollywood day-dream, while his grandmother's overriding trait is greed for rich food. Martin is, however, more fortunate than his school-friend Heinrich, whose mother is dependent on a succession of 'uncles' to support her and her two children. In this novel Böll ingeniously varies the scenes from urban life which he describes, from the synthetic glitter of prosperity to the shabbiness of the lives of ordinary lives. *Das Brot der frühen Jahre* ('The Bread of Early Years', 1955) is Böll's first extended love-story. A twenty-three-year-old mechanic who specializes in repairs to washing machines, falls in love at first sight. His actions during this fateful Monday are interspersed with flash-backs which explain his present mood in terms of earlier deprivations. As a schoolboy and in the early days of his apprenticeship he was constantly hungry, with an obsession for bread which embittered him and caused him to steal. Since then his life has been centred upon work for the sake of money and what money can buy.

Falling in love is shown as having a purifying effect, enabling him to make a new moral valuation of himself and others. In this story fantasy threatens to break through more insistently than in the earlier novels.

Böll's first volume of short stories (*Wanderer, kommst du nach Spa . . .*, 'Wanderer, if you come to Spa . . .', 1950) depicts war and its aftermath, for the most part with a grim pathos and indignation. As in the two first novels, the sheer force of the material moulds the manner of its expression. It is a type of writing which may owe something to Hemingway and has something in common with the sketches and stories of Borchert. In the best of them ('Über die Brücke', 'Over the Bridge'; 'Der Mann mit den Messern', 'The Man with the Knives') the suspense is maintained with striking effect. The story *Nicht nur zur Weihnachtszeit* ('Not only at Christmas Time', 1952) is a grim satire on the conventional celebration of Christmas by a middle-class family that is set on keeping up appearances at all costs. Later volumes of short stories (*So ward Abend und Morgen*, 'Evening and Morning', 1955; *Unberechenbare Gäste*, 'Incalculable Guests', 1956) and *Doktor Murkes gesammeltes Schweigen* ('Dr. Murke's Collected Silences', 1958) are still sharply satirical in content, but the shrill note of Böll's earlier protests has been replaced by a gentler and smoother tone and a more directly humorous effect. *Im Tal der donnernden Hufe* ('In the Valley of the Thundering Hoof', 1957) takes up the theme of adolescent violence and frustration; the tale is set against the background of a prosperous wine-producing Rhineland town. Böll's uneasiness at the busy prosperity of Western Germany since 1948 is reflected again in his *Irisches Tagebuch* ('Irish Diary', 1957), a travel book where he dwells lovingly on his impressions of a country which he contrasts with his own.

Böll's imagination is fertile and wide in scope. It seems as if almost any aspect of contemporary urban civilization which he encounters is capable of starting off an inventive sequence of fictional situations. He can make his reader see and feel the detail and background of his stories, and can create strong conflicts and tender human situations. Sharp satire with social and moral criticism shades off into light, sparkling comedy. His style is colloquial, assured in its familiarity with the language of mechanized living. There is no doubt about the vitality and promise of his writing and that of a number of his contemporaries.

XI

SUMMING UP

GERMAN fiction between 1945 and 1957 is full of variety and wide
in range; only a selection has been discussed here. In its subject-
matter there is no avoidance of major problems of a contemporary
nature. Many novelists have wished to make their reckoning
with the events of 1933-45, and have expressed in decided terms
their revulsion from the régime of that time. There has been in
particular among younger writers a desire to write about the
present and its problems in an uncompromising manner. One of
them, Krämer-Badoni, has put it like this:

If I pick up a novel which deals with the present time but makes a
détour round contemporary ideas, cares and horrors, obviously because
the author has in mind his possible readers of 1999, then I put the book
respectfully on one side. Unfortunately it was not written for me, for
by 1999 I shall have been dead a long time.

He who hovers above his time because he wants to do justice to
eternity confuses the never with the eternal.

There are no thoughts or works of lasting value at all apart from
those which arise shrewdly from the present day, which exist in the
present day and which are there with a vigorous blow for the present
day.

The *Zeitroman* which springs from such a programme hovers
uneasily between literature, reporting and confession. Many of
the works which have been mentioned are novels of ideas, and it
is true that the German novel-reader tolerates, even welcomes a
greater ballast of speculative thought in fiction than is usual in the
English novel; this is in the tradition of the *Bildungsroman*, with
its inevitably didactic tendency. Indeed it is remarkable how
persistent the influence of this long biographical novel form still
is in Germany; it forms the structure of works as different as

Mann's *Doktor Faustus*, Gertrud von Le Fort's *Das Schweißtuch der Veronika*, Hesse's *Das Glasperlenspiel* or Jahnn's *Fluß ohne Ufer*, to mention only a few. The emphasis on the gradual unfolding of the personality of one individual almost necessarily makes for a subjective, lyrical, introverted approach; we are concerned with the thoughts and feelings of one person in his reactions to the outside world. Many German novelists are more at home with this analytical type of writing than with the manipulation of a group of characters or a whole society seen in the round; Doderer's mastery in this latter respect is exceptional. The *Novelle* too remains formally satisfying, particularly when handled with skill as in the case of Bergengruen or Gertrud von Le Fort. The short story, it has been indicated previously, is an interesting newer development in modern German narrative prose.

While the traditionally German forms of narrative writing still exert considerable attraction, there has been a pronounced tendency to seek new models and to be willing to experiment. During the Nazi period experimental writing was frowned upon, if not forbidden absolutely, and the renewed interest in the psycho-analytical, surrealist approach that has been marked in Germany in the last few years is in part the revival of an outlook that goes back to the Expressionists and that has more recently made a renewed impact on a new generation. The revival of the stream of consciousness technique and the preoccupation with time and memory are aspects of the novel which have been receiving considerable attention in Germany recently, and the influence of Kafka, rediscovered by a generation to whom he had previously only been a name, has been extensive. Perhaps Surrealism should be regarded as a technique rather than a set attitude to life, for its influence is to be found in a number of authors who otherwise have little in common.

The technique of the inner monologue, or stream of consciousness, may be taken as the characteristic feature of the English experimental novel of the nineteen-twenties, rather as the letter-form gave fresh possibilities of expression to the eighteenth-century novel (one thinks of Richardson, Rousseau's *La nouvelle*

Héloïse or Goethe's *Werther*). The search for an all-embracing totality which shall include time, memory, history and myth, to be conducted through probing psychological analysis in a lyrical, non-realistic prose; this was the ambitious programme for the analytical novel. If English novelists have been returning to more traditional forms and have been using the methods of Joyce and Virginia Woolf more sparingly, as a technique that shall be subordinated to the more usual ways of story-telling, we find in Germany writers such as Broch, Jahnn and Langgässer taking up without qualification or misgivings the challenge of *Ulysses*. Indeed there is no reason why the experimental novel form of the nineteen-twenties should not appeal to the German writer who also looks back to the *Bildungsroman*. Proust and Joyce do after all take as their starting-point the individual stream of consciousness, and tend to filter the outside world through the viewpoint of a single mind; the subjective, analytical element is an important factor to them and to the German *Bildungsroman* tradition.

In reaction against the analytical approach was E. M. Forster's *Aspects of the Novel* (1928) with its insistence that the first task of the novelist is to tell a story. Whatever else a work of fiction may or may not do, he tells us, it must keep up the suspense of the narrative. The dramatic element, dependent upon the tension aroused by conflict, is essential, and to this psychological analysis should play at most a subordinate part. Edwin Muir made a similar plea in his *The Structure of the Novel* (1928), and Robert Liddell (*A Treatise on the Novel*, 1947) has demanded a stricter attention to the requirements of narrative form. Mann, for all his affinities to the analytical experimenters of the nineteen-twenties, assumed as a fundamental need for the novelist that he should make his narrative move forward—not perhaps in a straight line, but at least with a discernible thread linking the action from a beginning to an end in the world of common-sense experience; *Doktor Faustus* maintains its narrative suspense in spite of its complexity of symbolism and its learned divagations. Musil was much less successful in this respect, though conscious of the problem. As he is walking alone at night in the Ringstrasse in Vienna,

Musil's hero Ulrich meditates on the contrast between town and country. Life in the big city has a confusing many-sidedness and an apparent meaninglessness in its activity, while country life has a concrete significance which Ulrich then compares with the form of the traditional art of fiction:

It is the simple sequence, the reproduction of the overwhelming variety of life in a one-dimensional form, as a mathematician might say, that reassures us; the act of arranging everything that has happened in time or place on to a thread, in fact that famous thread of life. Happy the man who can say 'when', 'before', and 'after'! . . . Most people are in their fundamental relationship to themselves narrators. They do not like the lyrical, or only for short moments . . . They like the orderly arrangement of facts in sequence, because this makes it look like a form of necessity, and they feel somehow protected in the midst of chaos by the impression that their life has a 'course' to run. And Ulrich noticed that he had lost hold of this primitive epic sense which we cling to in private life, although in the wider sphere of public life everything has already become impossible to count and no longer follows a thread, but spreads out in an infinitely interwoven surface.

These words of Ulrich are one way of summing up the problem that faces the writer of experimental fiction of the inner monologue kind. In Germany it has been by and large the older generation of authors who have been the most radically experimental, while young authors have preferred the shorter novel form with a dramatic narrative manner. The adventure story, the document of an age of violence, is the form of fiction which these writers prefer, and in their artistic approach to the melodrama of life the figure of Hemingway has been influential; it is an approach which is not necessarily inconsistent with the traditional German *Novelle*. In the short story the combination of fantasy, poetry, satire, and wit has been increasingly essayed and has become an additional distinguishing factor in recent German writing.

German fiction since 1945 may have certain unevennesses in quality, but it is lively and interesting both in its themes and formal tendencies. We find here a direct encountering of the issues of the time, an openness to stimuli from all directions, yet a continuity with earlier German narrative traditions, revealed particularly in the tension between inner and outer realities and a desire to write seriously; there is much that is independent, vigorous and thoughtful.

SELECT BIBLIOGRAPHY

ALKER, ERNST, *Geschichte der deutschen Literatur von Goethes Tod bis zur Gegenwart.* Stuttgart, 1949 50.

ASTON, S. C., and TOPSFIELD, L. T. (general editors), *The Year's Work in Modern Language Studies.* Vols. 11–18 (for studies appearing 1940–56), Cambridge, 1951–7.

BAIER, CLAIR, 'German Literary and Linguistic Publications during the War Years 1939–1944'. *Modern Language Review*, vol. 42, 1947 (further lists in subsequent vols.).

BENNETT, E. K., *A History of the German Novelle from Goethe to Thomas Mann.* Cambridge, 1934.

BETTEX, ALBERT, *The German Novel of Today.* Cambridge, 1939.

BETTEX, ALBERT, *Die Literatur der deutschen Schweiz von heute.* n.d.

BITHELL, JETHRO (editor), *Germany: A Companion to German Studies.* 4th ed., 1955.

BITHELL, JETHRO, *Modern German Literature, 1880–1938.* 1939.

BOESCHENSTEIN, H., *The German Novel, 1939–1944.* Toronto, 1949.

CLOSS, AUGUST, *Medusa's Mirror,* 1957.

CYSARZ, HERBERT, 'Unsere Weltwende im Roman der großen Literaturen'. In: *Forschungsprobleme der Vergleichenden Literaturgeschichte.* Tübingen, 1950.

DODERER, KLAUS, *Die Kurzgeschichte in Deutschland. Ihre Form und ihre Entwicklung.* Wiesbaden, 1953.

DODERER, KLAUS, 'Die Kurzgeschichte als literarische Form'. *Wirkendes Wort,* vol. 8, 1957.

EPPELSHEIMER, HANNS W. (editor), *Bibliographie der deutschen Literaturwissenschaft 1945–1953.* Frankfurt, 1957, vol. 2, 1954–1956. (Edited by Clemens Köttelwesch), Frankfurt, 1958.

FORSTER, LEONARD, *German Poetry 1944–1948.* Cambridge, 1949.

FRIEDMANN, HERMANN, and MANN, OTTO (editors), *Deutsche Literatur im zwanzigsten Jahrhundert.* Heidelberg, 1954.

FRIEDMANN, HERMANN, and MANN, OTTO (editors), *Christliche Dichter der Gegenwart.* Heidelberg, 1955.

GRENZMANN, WILHELM, *Dichtung und Glaube.* 2nd ed., Bonn, 1952.

GRENZMANN, WILHELM, *Deutsche Dichtung der Gegenwart.* Frankfurt, 1953.

Select Bibliography

HELLER, ERICH, *The Disinherited Mind*. Cambridge, 1952.

HOLTHUSEN, HANS EGON, *Der unbehauste Mensch. Motive und Probleme der modernen Literatur*. Munich, 1951.

HORST, K. A., *Die deutsche Literatur der Gegenwart*. Munich, 1957.

KESTEN, HERMANN (editor), *Unsere Zeit. Die schönsten Erzählungen des zwanzigsten Jahrhunderts*. Cologne, 1956.

KINDERMANN, HEINZ (editor), *Wegweiser durch die moderne Literatur in Österreich*. Innsbruck, 1954.

KLEIN, JOHANNES, *Geschichte der deutschen Novelle von Goethe bis zur Gegenwart*. 2nd ed., Wiesbaden, 1954.

KOSCH, WILHELM (editor), *Deutsches Literatur-Lexikon*. 2nd ed., Berne, 1949– .

KUNZ, JOSEPH, 'Geschichte der deutschen Novelle vom 18. Jahrhundert bis auf die Gegenwart'. In: *Deutsche Philologie im Aufriß*. Berlin, Bielefeld and Munich, vol. 2, 1954.

KUTZBACH, KARL AUGUST (editor), *Autorenlexikon der Gegenwart*. Bonn, 1950.

LANGE, VICTOR, *Modern German Literature 1870–1940*. Ithaca, New York, 1945.

LENNARTZ, FRANZ, *Dichter und Schriftsteller unserer Zeit*. 6th ed., Stuttgart, 1954.

MAJUT, RUDOLF, 'Geschichte des deutschen Romans vom Biedermeier bis zur Gegenwart'. In: *Deutsche Philologie im Aufriß*. Berlin, Bielefeld and Munich, vol. 2, 1954.

MARTIN, JACQUES, 'Romans et romanciers de l'Allemagne d'aprèsguerre'. *Etudes Germaniques*, Paris and Lyons, vol. 8, 1953.

MARTINI, FRITZ, 'Deutsche Literatur zwischen 1880 and 1950. Ein Forschungsbericht'. *Deutsche Vierteljahrsschrift*, vol. 26, 1952.

MARTINI, FRITZ, *Deutsche Literaturgeschichte von den Anfängen bis zur Gegenwart*. 4th ed., Stuttgart, 1952.

MARTINI, FRITZ, *Das Wagnis der Sprache. Interpretationen deutscher Prosa von Nietzsche bis Benn*. Stuttgart, 1954.

MILCH, WERNER, *Ströme, Formeln, Manifeste. Drei Vorträge zur Geschichte der deutschen Literatur im 20. Jahrhundert*. Marburg, 1949.

MORGAN, BAYARD QUINCY, *A Critical Bibliography of German Literature in English Translation*. 2nd ed., California, 1938.

MUSCHG, WALTER, *Die Zerstörung der deutschen Literatur*. Berne, 1956.

PASCAL, ROY, *The German Novel*. Manchester, 1956.

SAMUEL, RICHARD, and THOMAS, R. HINTON, *Expressionism in German Life, Literature and the Theatre, 1910–1924.* Cambridge, 1939.

ULSHÖFER, ROBERT (editor), 'Die Kurzgeschichte im Unterricht'. *Der Deutschunterricht,* vol. 9, 1957.

WAIDSON, H. M., 'Experiment and Tradition. Some German Fiction since 1945'. *German Life and Letters,* New Series, vol. 7, 1954.

WAIDSON, H. M., *German Short Stories 1945–1955.* Cambridge, 1957.

WAIDSON, H. M., 'Der moderne Roman in England und Deutschland'. *Wirkendes Wort,* vol. 7, 1957.

WAIDSON, H. M., 'Zeitgenössische deutsche Literatur in englischer Übersetzung'. *Pädagogische Blätter,* vol. 7, 1956; reprinted in *Deutschunterricht für Ausländer,* vol. 8, 1958.

WAIDSON, H. M., 'The Recent German Novel'. In: *International Literary Annual, No. 1* (ed. John Wain), 1958.

WIESE, BENNO VON, *Die deutsche Novelle von Goethe bis Kafka.* Düsseldorf, 1956.

ZIMMERMANN, WERNER, *Deutsche Prosadichtung der Gegenwart. Interpretationen für Lehrende und Lernende.* Düsseldorf, 1954–6.

Books and essays on individual authors have not been included here, but a number of the bibliographical works listed above supply detailed information.

LIST OF AUTHORS AND WORKS

THIS list of prose narrative works is in general restricted to those titles mentioned in the preceding pages which were first published between 1945 and 1957. Where they are known to be available, titles and dates of English translations and names of the translators are indicated in brackets.

AICHINGER, ILSE: *Die größere Hoffnung*, 1948.
Der Gefesselte, 1953 (*The Bound Man*, Eric Mosbacher, 1955).
ALBERS, HEINZ: *Landung ohne Ankunft*, 1957.
ANDRES, STEFAN: *Wir sind Utopia*, 1942 (*We Are Utopia*, Cyrus Brook, 1954).
Die Hochzeit der Feinde, 1947.
Ritter der Gerechtigkeit, 1948.
Die Sintflut. Vol. 1, *Das Tier aus der Tiefe*, 1949; vol. 2, *Die Arche*, 1951.
Die Reise nach Portiuncula, 1954.
BECHER, JOHANNES R.: *Abschied*, 1948.
BENDER, HANS: *Wölfe und Tauben*, 1957.
BENN, GOTTFRIED: *Der Ptolemäer*, 1949.
BERGENGRUEN, WERNER: *Das Beichtsiegel*, 1946.
Der Sternenstand, 1947.
Pelageja, 1947.
Das Feuerzeichen, 1949.
Der letzte Rittmeister, 1952 (*The Last Captain of Horse*, Eric Peters, 1953).
Die Rittmeisterin, 1954.
Die Flamme im Säulenholz, 1955.
BÖLL, HEINRICH: *Der Zug war pünktlich*, 1949 (*The Train Was on Time*, Richard Graves, 1956).
Wo warst du, Adam, 1950 (*Adam, Where Art Thou?*, Mervyn Savill, 1955).
Wanderer, kommst du nach Spa . . . , 1950 (*Traveller, If You Come to Spa*, Mervyn Savill, 1956).

Und sagte kein einziges Wort, 1953 *(Acquainted With the Night,* Richard Graves, 1955).

Haus ohne Hüter, 1954 *(The Unguarded House,* Mervyn Savill, 1957).

Das Brot der frühen Jahre, 1955 *(The Bread of Our Early Years,* Mervyn Savill, 1957).

So ward Abend und Morgen, 1955.

Unberechenbare Gäste, 1956.

Im Tal der donnernden Hufe, 1957.

Doktor Murkes Gesammeltes Schweigen, 1958; this volume includes *Nicht nur zur Weihnachtszeit,* 1952.

BORCHERT, WOLFGANG: *Das Gesamtwerk,* 1949 *(The Man Outside. The Prose Works of Wolfgang Borchert,* David Porter, 1952).

BRECHT, BERTOLT: *Kalendergeschichten,* 1949.

BREDEL, WILLI: *Verwandte und Bekannte.* Vol. 1, *Die Väter,* 1943; vol. 2, *Die Söhne,* 1954; vol. 3, *Die Enkel,* 1956.

BROCH, HERMANN: *Der Tod des Vergil,* 1945 *(The Death of Virgil,* Jean Starr Untermeyer, 1946).

Die Schuldlosen, 1950.

Der Versucher, 1953.

BURCKHARDT, CARL J.: *Drei Erzählungen,* 1952.

CAROSSA, HANS: *Ungleiche Welten,* 1951.

Der Tag des jungen Arztes, 1955.

DÖBLIN, ALFRED: *November 1918. Eine deutsche Revolution.* 4 vols. 1939–50.

DODERER, HEIMITO VON: *Die Strudlhofstiege,* 1951.

Das letzte Abenteuer, 1953.

Die Dämonen, 1956.

DÜRRENMATT, FRIEDRICH: *Der Verdacht,* 1953.

Der Richter und sein Henker, 1952 *(The Judge and His Hangman,* Cyrus Brooks, 1954).

EDSCHMID, KASIMIR: *Das gute Recht,* 1946.

Der Zauberfaden, 1949.

Wenn es Rosen sind, werden sie blühen, 1950.

EISENREICH, HERBERT, *Böse schöne Welt,* 1957.

FRISCH, MAX: *Stiller,* 1954 *(I'm not Stiller,* Michael Bullock, 1958).

GAISER, GERD: *Eine Stimme hebt an,* 1950.

Die sterbende Jagd, 1953 *(The Falling Leaf,* Paul Findlay, 1956).

Das Schiff im Berg, 1953.

Einmal und oft, 1957.

Schlußball, 1958.

GOES, ALBRECHT: *Unruhige Nacht*, 1949 (*Arrow to the Heart*, Constantine Fitzgibbon, 1951).

Das Brandopfer, 1954 (*The Burnt Offering*, Michael Hamburger, 1956).

GRAF, OSKAR MARIA: *Die Eroberung einer Welt*, 1948.

GUGGENHEIM, KURT: *Der Friede des Herzens*, 1956.

HEINRICH, WILLI: *Das geduldige Fleisch*, 1955 (*The Willing Flesh*, Richard and Clara Winston, 1956).

HEISELER, BERNT VON: *Versöhnung*, 1953.

HESSE, HERMANN: *Das Glasperlenspiel*, 1943 (*Magister Ludi*, Mervyn Savill, 1950).

HESSE, MAX RENÉ: *Dietrich Kattenburg*. Vol. 1, *Dietrich und der Herr der Welt*, 1937; vol. 2, *Jugend ohne Stern*, 1943; vol. 3, *Überreife Zeit*, 1950.

HEUSCHELE, OTTO: *Musik durchbricht die Nacht*, 1956.

HILDESHEIMER, WOLFGANG: *Ich trage eine Eule nach Athen*, 1956.

IHLENFELD, KURT: *Wintergewitter*, 1951.

Kommt wieder, Menschenkinder, 1954.

INGLIN, MEINRAD: *Die Lawine*, 1947.

Werner Amberg, 1949.

JAHNN, HANS HENNY: *Fluß ohne Ufer*. Vol. 1, *Das Holzschiff*, 1937; vols. 2 and 3, *Die Niederschrift des Gustav Anias Horn*, 1949, 1950.

JENS, WALTER: *Nein. Die Welt der Angeklagten*, 1950.

Der Blinde, 1951 (*The Blind Man*, Michael Bullock, 1954).

Vergessene Gesichter, 1952.

Der Mann, der nicht alt werden wollte, 1955.

JÜNGER, ERNST: *Auf den Marmorklippen*, 1939 (*On the Marble Cliffs*, Stuart Hood, 1947).

Heliopolis, 1949.

Besuch auf Godenholm, 1952.

Gläserne Bienen, 1957.

KASACK, HERMANN: *Die Stadt hinter dem Strom*, 1947 (*The City Beyond the River*, Peter de Mendelssohn, 1953).

Das große Netz, 1952.

KESTEN, HERMANN: *Die Zwillinge von Nürnberg*, 1947.

KIRST, HANS HELLMUT: *Null-acht-fünfzehn*, 3 vols. 1954–5 (*Zero Eight Fifteen*, Robert Kee, 3 vols. 1955–7).

KRÄMER-BADONI, RUDOLF: *In der großen Drift*, 1949.

Der arme Reinhold, 1951.

Die Insel hinter dem Vorhang, 1955.

KREUDER, ERNST: *Die Gesellschaft vom Dachboden,* 1946 (*The Attic Pretenders,* Robert Kee, 1948).

Die Unauffindbaren, 1948.

Herein ohne anzuklopfen, 1954.

KÜBLER, ALFRED, *Öppi.* Vol. 1, *Öppi von Wasenwachs,* 1943; vol. 2, *Öppi der Student,* 1947; vol. 3, *Öppi und Eva,* 1951.

KUSENBERG, KURT: *Die Sonnenblumen,* 1951.

Wein auf Lebenszeit, 1955.

LAMPE, FRIEDO: *Das Gesamtwerk,* 1955.

LANDGREBE, ERICH: *Mit dem Ende beginnt es,* 1951.

In sieben Tagen, 1955.

LANGGÄSSER, ELISABETH: *Das unauslöschliche Siegel,* 1946.

Der Torso, 1947.

Märkische Argonautenfahrt, 1950.

LE FORT, GERTRUD VON: *Das Schweißtuch der Veronika.* Vol. 1, *Der römische Brunnen,* 1928 (*The Veil of Veronica,* Conrad M. R. Bonacina, 1932); vol. 2, *Der Kranz der Engel,* 1946.

Die Tochter Farinatas, 1950.

Gelöschte Kerzen, 1953.

Am Tor des Himmels, 1954.

Die Frau des Pilatus, 1955.

Der Turm der Beständigkeit, 1957.

LENZ, SIEGFRIED: *So zärtlich war Suleyken,* 1955.

MANN, THOMAS: *Doktor Faustus,* 1947 (*Doctor Faustus,* H. T. Lowe-Porter, 1949).

Der Erwählte, 1951 (*The Holy Sinner,* H. T. Lowe-Porter, 1952).

Die Betrogene, 1953 (*The Black Swan,* W. R. Trask, 1954).

Die Bekenntnisse des Hochstaplers Felix Krull, 1954 (*Confessions of Felix Krull, Confidence Man,* Denver Lindley, 1955).

MEICHSNER, DIETER: *Weisst du warum?,* 1952 (*Vain Glory,* Charlotte and A. L. Lloyd, 1953).

MUSIL, ROBERT: *Der Mann ohne Eigenschaften,* 1930–42. German edition of Robert Frisé, 1952 (*The Man Without Qualities,* Eithne Wilkins and Ernst Kaiser, 1953–   ).

NOSSACK, HANS ERICH: *Nekyia. Bericht eines Überlebenden,* 1947.

Dorothea, 1948.

Spätestens im November, 1955.

Der jüngere Bruder, 1958.

List of Authors and Works

PLIEVIER, THEODOR: *Stalingrad,* 1946 (*Stalingrad,* H. Langmead Robinson, 1948).

Moskau, 1952 (*Moscow,* Stuart Hood, 1953).

Berlin, 1954 (*Berlin,* Louis Hagen and Vivian Milroy, 1956).

POHL, GERHART: *Wieviel Mörder gibt es?,* 1953.

REMARQUE, ERICH MARIA: *Arc de Triomphe,* 1946 (*Arch of Triumph,* Walter Sorell and Denver Lindley, 1946).

RICHTER, HANS WERNER: *Die Geschlagenen,* 1949 (*The Odds Against Us,* Robert Kee, 1950).

Sie fielen aus Gottes Hand, 1951 (*They Fell From God's Hand,* Geoffrey Sainsbury, 1956).

Du sollst nicht töten, 1955.

RINSER, LUISE: *Mitte des Lebens,* 1950.

Daniela, 1953.

Der Sündenbock, 1955.

Ein Bündel weißer Narzissen, 1956; this volume includes *Jan Lobel aus Warschau,* 1948.

RISSE, HEINZ: *Irrfahrer,* 1948.

Wenn die Erde bebt, 1950 (*The Earthquake,* Rita Eldon, 1953).

So frei von Schuld, 1951.

Belohne dich selbst, 1953.

Dann kam der Tag, 1953.

Simson und die kleinen Leute, 1954.

SCHAPER, EDZARD: *Die Freiheit der Gefangenen,* 1949.

Die Macht der Ohnmächtigen, 1951.

SCHMIDT, ARNO: *Leviathan,* 1949.

Brand's Haide, 1951.

Aus dem Leben eines Fauns, 1953.

SCHNURRE, WOLFDIETRICH: *Sternstaub und Sänfte,* 1953.

Eine Rechnung, die nicht aufgeht, 1958.

SEGHERS, ANNA: *Die Toten bleiben jung,* 1949 (*The Dead Stay Young,* 1950).

Der Bienenstock, 2 vols., 1956.

STEPHAN, HANNA: *Engel, Menschen und Dämonen,* 1952; this volume includes *Der Dritte.*

UHSE, BODO: *Wir Söhne,* 1947.

Die Patrioten. Vol. 1, *Abschied und Heimkehr,* 1954.

WALTER, HANS: *Im Verborgenen,* 1950.

WARSINSKY, WERNER: *Kimmerische Fahrt,* 1953.

WERFEL, FRANZ: *Stern der Ungeborenen*, 1945.

Erzählungen aus zwei Welten, 3 vols., 1948–54.

WIECHERT, ERNST: *Die Jerominkinder*, 1945–7 (*The Earth Is Our Heritage*, Robert Maxwell, 1951).

Missa sine Nomine, 1950 (*Missa sine Nomine*, Marie Heynemann and Margery B. Ledward, 1953).

ZWEIG, ARNOLD: *Das Beil von Wandsbek*, 1947 (*The Axe of Wandsbek*, Eric Sutton, 1948).

INDEX

PRINTED IN GREAT BRITAIN
BY BUTLER AND TANNER LIMITED
FROME AND LONDON